HUMAN RESOURCE MANAGEMENT AFTER GLOBALISATION

HUMAN RESOURCE MANAGEMENT AFTER GLOBALISATION

By
Dr. Rabi Narayana Misra

DISCOVERY PUBLISHING HOUSE PVT. LTD.
NEW DELHI-110 002

Reprinted - 2019

First Published - 2009

ISBN: 978-81-8536-467-0

Human Resource Management After Globalisation

Published by:

DISCOVERY PUBLISHING HOUSE PVT. LTD.

4383/4B, Ansari Road, Darya Ganj

New Delhi-110 002 (India)

Phone: +91-11-23279245, 43596064-65

Fax: +91-11-23253475

E-mail: discoverypublishinghouse@gmail.com

sales@discoverypublishinggroup.com

web: www.discoverypublishinggroup.com

Printed at:

Infinity Imaging Systems

Delhi

Preface

Human Resource Management (HRM) is a management function that helps managers to recruit, select, train and develop members for an organisation. HRM is concerned with the people's dimension in organisation. HRM plays an important source or asset to be used for the benefit of organisation, employees and the society. It is emerging as a distinct philosophy of management aiming at policies that promote mutuality—mutual goals, mutual respect, mutual rewards and mutual responsibilities. HRM cannot be treated in isolation. It is being integrated into the overall strategic management of business in present era.

After globalisation, business organisations have realised that the need of the hour is to have skilled, well-trained and highly motivated staff to help with the growth of the organisation. Each business organisation invests time and money for the welfare and benefit of the employees, because they see merit in such activities. In present business scenario HRM has looked as a safety cap, which would involve smoothening of relations between management and workers. For the growth and development of any business organisation HRM is very essential and need due consideration.

Acknowledgement

I am very much thankful to all paper contributors of this book. It is not possible in my part to edit this book without their help and co-operation.

A very special thanks to my wife Smt. Swarna Prava, my sons Roopesh and Rokesh, and also to my daughter-in-law Amrita Rani Misra, lecturer in English, for their timely help and encouragement to edit this book.

I express my sincere gratitude to Mr. Tilak Wasan, the Director, Discovery Publishing House Pvt. Ltd., New Delhi, his son Parul, and all the staff members of Discovery Publishing House for their kind help and co-operation in publishing the book on time.

Dr. Rabi N. Misra

Contents

Human Resource Management After Globalisation

Competency Mapping

Ipsita Kar♣
R.N. Misra♠

INTRODUCTION

In the good old days, the generic term for "staffing "functions within organisations was "personnel". However, at that time, the "personnel" department looked after purely administrative tasks, such as dispatching salary cheques or drafting letters of appreciation. With companies setting shop all over the world, there is an increased level of understanding for the need of better management of an organisation's most valuable resource—its people.

With globalisation, organisations have realised that the need of the hour is to have skilled, well-trained and highly motivated staff to help with the growth of the company. Organisations invest time and money for the welfare and

♣ Miss Ipsita Kar, Final year MBA student, PGCMS, SMIT, Ankushpur (Berhampur).

♠ Dr. R.N. Misra, Professor MBA, PGCMS, SMIT, Ankushpur (Berhampur).

benefit of the employees because they see merit in such activities. All this and more has led this part of an organisations activity to be called Human Resource Management (HRM). However, there is more to HRM than just being an internal function of a corporate. Since the dawn of the corporate era HR departments have been relegated to the background with no say whatsoever in the board room. They were merely passive administrators charged with tactical transactions and implementation of policy decisions. All of a sudden, though every one is talking about "strategic HR".

The routine activities of recruitment, compensation, benefits, rewards and training are acquiring a bigger dimension. Just about two decades back, all that HR was looked at was a safety cap, which would involve smoothening of relations between management and workers. From industrial relations, HR has undergone transformational change and now is more of a strategic requirement of any organisation It is no more a bunch of people who would sit and calculate salaries, leaves, it is now a tool to look, understand performances and resource planning. Through HR, companies go for manpower planning which is more than just required for the companies to survive in the highly competitive world. Besides, counselling and other HR supportive functions are used to get the best out of each person that an organisation have employed and thus help it in getting maximum return on investment on each employee.

In the globalised business scenario, all companies are encouraging high performance culture. The pervasive change in technology is a major contributing factor to skill shortage, with skills going obsolete in less than the time it takes to learn them business leaders view skills shortage in the future as their biggest barriers to success . With a glut of new career options being thrown open by the economy and the massive exodus of locally available talent to greener pastures abroad, many industries are facing an acute skill shortage. The question is whether it is just another buzz word in the HR block or is there something momentous beyond the type? Will the HR function live up to the hoopla and turn into a source of competitive advantage, or will it collapse under its own weight as more and more responsibilities are piled on to it? Today's global economy is slowly waking up to the fact that harnessing human assets is critical for organisations striving to function at a higher level and achieve perpetual success. This calls for integrating human capital considerations in to daily decision-making and planning. Consequently, HR strategy right from benefits to training to retention needs to be in sync with overall business objective. By virtue of its unique position to the work force, HR has earned a prominent seat at the executive table. The HR fraternity is gaining importance and moving to a wider role as a 'strategic business partner' in line with other core functions. It is no longer a mere reactive implementer, but plays a more proactive role participating in the strategy formulation process.

SCOPE AND OBJECTIVE

HRM plays an important role after globalisation. High performance culture is considered significant in the present scenario. For this purpose competency mapping, which now considered by the different organisation of the country as important factor for the development of HRM strategies, is given due importance in this study. For the study purpose only published data are taken, so all the limitation of secondary data are found in this study.

HRM STRATEGIES

Strategic HRM has been defined as, "The linking of HR with strategic goals and objectives in order to improve business performance and develop an organisational culture that fosters innovation and flexibility".

Whilst organisations are accepting (albeit grudgingly) the HR function as a partner in business operations, HR managers can no longer afford to be in the middle of the road. They have to rise to the bait and contribute to business improvement helping organisations achieve their goals.

Leading consultant, Siddhartha Chaturvedi exhorts the new leadership role as, "A strategic perspective of HRM requires simultaneous consideration of both external (business strategy) and internal (consistency) requirement leading to superior performance of the firm".

To become a true business differentiator, HR should not only be involved in policy-making and implementation responsibilities, but also translate them into HR priorities. They should design HR initiatives and practices that synergise business strategy with employment planning. They should realise that they are well placed to recognise and exploit external opportunities.

HR departments also have to add value to the business by mobilising and managing the most important resource—its people. They should work towards effectively utilising the full potential of their human capital to gain a performance advantage. They should shape critical HR interventions for tapping the organisation's core competencies, maximising current capabilities, identifying future staffing needs and creating organisational abilities.

For that, strategic HR is all about facilitating and enhancing organisational goals. Towards this end, HR should:

- Harness its knowledge of the company's internal strengths and weaknesses to supply competitive intelligence for planning purposes;
- Identify business needs and step up to the strategy table with new ideas;
- Apply cutting-edge thinking to engage company executives in thought-provoking questions;
- Activate resources that support the chosen business strategy and implement it effectively;
- Ensure that the work force is engaged, excited, energised as well as capable of responding to organisational objectives in an efficient manner;

- Stir people to action and develop the next-generation leaders from the rank-and-file;
- Leverage individual talent and collective competencies to invent sustainable and distinct competitive advantages.

As good to great author Jim Collins says, "It's all about putting the right people on the right bus in the right seats at the right time".

Top HR director, Dana Jervis highlights, "This powerful tool leverages significant opportunities for HR departments to get the job done in not only an acceptable way, but an exceptional way thus positioning them for ..."

India should explore our competitive advantage which no other country has as 60 per cent of our population is below 20 years. A huge talent pool can be created by providing gainful productive employment. HR utilisation index of India is very poor and ranked above 100 in the world. HR strategies in big companies are now giving thrust to Total Productive Maintenance (TPM) as a way of life and shifting from fixed to variable pay by undertaking competency mapping.

GENERAL COMPETENCY MAPPING

Recruiting right kind of' skilled talent and their retention has become a matter of concern. Employee engagement and energising them is the key driver of organisational performance. Since the education system is not equipped to keep pace with the more complex manpower needs, HR personnel have been busy managing the readiness index of employees through competency analysis. The components of competency are:

1. Knowledge
2. Skills
3. Attitudes
4. Motives and Traits
5. Self Concept

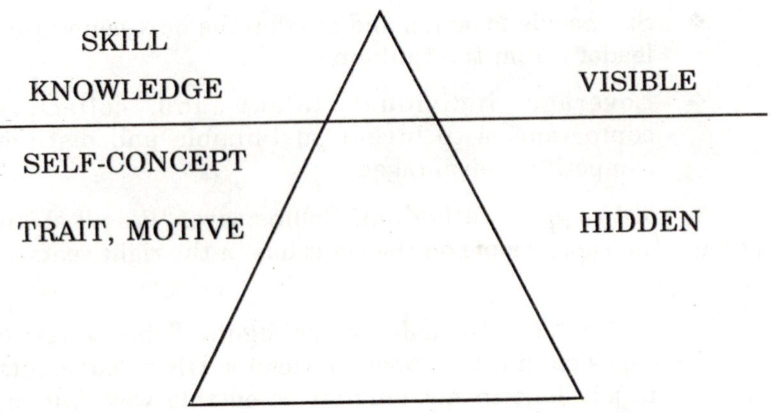

Knowledge

1. Knowledge consists of awareness and information which a person can acquire from various sources like books, websites, listening to others, television, newspapers, magazines etc.
2. It is cognitive competency and deals with what a person knows.
3. However, knowledge by itself is not sufficient to carry out an occupation or task. Knowledge on any subject only provides information.

Skills

1. It is the ability to actually perform a physical or mental task.
2. It requires co-ordination of the body and mind.
3. Skill to perform also requires knowledge, attitude and practice.
4. Some examples are:
   - *(a)* Skill to drive a bicycle or a car or an airplane;
   - *(b)* Skill to convince another person to buy a product;
   - *(c)* Skill to negotiate and get the product in the interest of the organisation.

Attitudes

1. They are predisposed to other individuals, groups, objects, situations, events and issues.
2. These are formed with experience.
3. They need not remain the same and are likely to change.
4. Attitudes can be positive or negative.
5. Attitudes influence the approach.

Values

1. Values are more enduring and generalised belief.
2. They are more permanent in nature than attitudes.
3. They are learnt from family, peers, organisation and society.
4. Some examples: Honesty, Openness, Transparency, Occupational values, Integrity etc.

Motives and Traits

1. The things a person constantly thinks or wants, that cause action are called "Motives".
2. Traits include physical qualities or characteristics like quick reaction time, good eyesight for drivers etc.

Self Concept

1. This constitutes a person's image of him/herself including the self worth, confidence and attitude to one's self-things one values, qualities one possess, goals one achieved.
2. E.g. Self confidence.
3. A person's belief that he/she can be effective in almost any situation is a part of the individual's self-concept.

TECHNICAL COMPETENCY MAPPING

The following methods are used in combination with competency mapping: Interviews, Group work, Task Forces,

Task Analysis Workshops, Questionnaire, Use of Job Descriptions, Performance Appraisal Formats etc.

(a) How are they identified?

The process of identification is not very complex. Some of the methods are given below:

- Simply ask each person who is currently performing the role to list the tasks to be performed by him one by one and identify the Knowledge, Attitude and Skills required performing each of them. Consolidate the list, present it to a role set group or a special task force constituted for that role, Edit and Finalise;
- Appoint a task force for each role.

(b) What language to use?

Use Technical Language for technical competencies. For e.g. Knowledge of hydraulics. Use business language for business competencies. E.g. Knowledge of markets for business or Strategic thinking. Use your own language or standard terms for behavior competencies. E.g. Ability to Negotiate, Interpersonal, Sensitivity, Sales techniques. Too technical and conceptual knowledge align to the organisation and people may create more problems than help.

(c) Who can do it?

Competency mapping is a task, which can be done by many people. Now-a-days all management schools and definitely those specialising in HR train the students in competency mapping. Any Master in Management or Social Sciences or an employee with equivalent experience and training can develop these competencies.

Conceptual background and understanding of the business is important. Familiarity with business, organisations, nanagement and behavioural sciences are useful. HR managers, management graduates, applied psychologists are quite qualified to do this. Most institutions specialising in HR train the candidates to do this.

Some tips on how to do it?

The following are some of tips to do competency mapping at low cost:

- ❖ Pick-up a job or a role that is relatively well understood by all individuals in the company. Work out for this role and give it as an illustration. For example Sales Executive, Production Supervisors, Assistant HR Manager, Receptionist, Transport Manager, PR Managers, are known to all and easy to profile;
- ❖ Work out competency for this role if necessary with the help of job analysis specialist or an internal member who has knowledge or competency mapping. Prepare this as an illustration;
- ❖ Circulate these to others and ask various departments to do it on their own;
- ❖ Circulate samples of competencies done by others;
- ❖ Illustrate knowledge, attitudes, skills, values etc.;
- ❖ Choose a sample that does not use jargons;
- ❖ Explain the purpose;
- ❖ Interview of past successful job holders helps;
- ❖ Current incumbent who are doing a good job along with their reporting officers is a good enough team in most cases;
- ❖ Once prepared even on the basis of one or two individuals' inputs, circulate to other role set members;
- ❖ Have a clear organisational structure;
- ❖ Well-defined roles in terms of the tasks and activities associated with each role;
- ❖ Should have mapped the competency required for each role;

- Where appropriate or needed should have identified the generic competency for each set of roles or levels of management;
- And should use them for recruitment, performance, management, promotion decisions and placement and training need identification.

CONCLUSION

Competency mapping is essentially an in-house job. Consultants can at best give the methodology and train of the line managers and HR staff. Consultants cannot do competency mapping all by themselves because no consultant can ever have all the knowledge required to identify the technological, managerial, human relations and other conceptual knowledge, attitudes and skills required for all jobs in a firm. Where consultants are excessively relied upon the data generated are likely to enrich the consultants and consulting firms much more than the commissioning firm itself.

The lower the consultant's involvement more the work needs to be done internally and higher the intellectual capital generation and retention within the organisation.

REFERENCES

1. *Personnel Management* by C.B. Memoria.
2. *Human Resource Management* by P. Suba Rao.
3. *Human Resource Management* by C.B. Gupta.
4. *HR Manual* NALCO.
5. *NALCO Journal*.

2

HRM Practices *After Globalisation*

Roopesh Kumar Misra[♣]
Rabi N. Misra[♠]

INTRODUCTION

The current financial crisis, which has engulfed East Asia since July 1997 and has subsequently spread to Russia and Brazil, is one of the most pressing challenges facing countries and businesses in today's global business environment. Most of the response to the financial crisis has focussed on macro-economic aspects and there is relatively little research on the role of human resources. Secondly, the issue of globalisation has been addressed predominantly in, and with respect to, the developed economies of Western Europe, North America and Japan. This paper is an attempt to address these two limitations since the human factor is one of the key issues in the new era of globalisation (Hassan, 1992; Sims and Sims, 1995). The primary objective of this paper therefore is to present a conceptual framework for strategic management

♣ Mr. R.K. Misra is a Research Scholar, Email: rupeshmisra@gmail.com
♠ Dr. Rabi N. Misra, Professor, MBA, SMIT, Ankuspur, Berhampur.

of human resources as a response to the growing interaction of globalisation and business performance.

Three central arguments made in this paper are: (1) That a great deal of evidence has accrued to suggest that changes taking place in the global business environment often are not accompanied by complementary changes in human resource management practices leading to a situation whereby the failure of some firms is due to the mismanagement of people rather than to problems with technical systems per se. (2) That this is because organisations have achieved relatively low levels of effectiveness in implementing Strategic Human Resource Management (SHRM) practices (Huselid, et al., 1997). This is particularly the case in emerging economies of South East Asia like Malaysia and other developing countries like Nigeria that are exposed to the challenges and opportunities of globalisation. (3) That in order to manage employees for competitive edge in a period of globalisation, human resource personnel must possess competencies relevant for effective implementation of such strategic HRM policies and practices (Barney and Wright, 1988; Cunningham and Debrah, 1995; Huselid, et al., 1997; Ulrich, 1987, 1996; Ulrich, et al., 1995). Following Wright and McMahan's (1992) comprehensive theoretical framework for SHRM, this paper develops competency-based research framework and draws implications for the strategic management of human resources to prepare organisations for the challenges of globalisation.

HRM ISSUES AND CHALLENGES GLOBAL MARAKETS

In coming 21st century, globalisation poses distinctive HRM challenges to businesses especially those operating across national boundaries as multinational or global enterprises. Global business is characterised by the free flow of human and financial resources especially in the developed economies of European Union (EU), the North American Free Trade Agreement (NAFTA), other regional groupings such as the Association of South East Asian Nations (ASEAN), the

Economic Community of West African States (ECOWAS), the Southern African Development Community, etc. These developments are opening up new markets in a way that has never been seen before. This accentuates the need to manage human resources effectively to gain competitive advantage in the global market place. To achieve this, organisations require an understanding of the factors that can determine the effectiveness of various HR practices and approaches. This is because countries differ along a number of dimensions that influence the attractiveness of Direct Foreign Investments in each country. These differences determine the economic viability of building an operation in a foreign country and they have a particularly strong impact on HRM in that operation. A number of factors that affect HRM in global markets are identified: (1) Culture (2) Economic System (3) Political System - the legal framework and (4) Human capital (Noe, et al, 2000: 536). (5) Social environment and various factors the scope of the present paper, only one dimension is treated: human capital (the skills, capabilities or competencies of the workforce). This is in consonance with the believe that competency-based human resource plans provide a source for gaining competitive advantage and for countries profoundly affect a foreign country's desire to locate or enter that country's market (O'Reilly, 1992). This partly explains why Japan and US locate and enter the local markets in South East Asia and Mexico respectively.

In the case of developing countries, globalisation poses distinct challenges to governments, the private sector and organised labour. These challenges, which must be addressed through a strategic approach to human resource management, include (1) Partnership in economic recovery especially in South East Asia (2) Dealing with the "big boys", the fund managers (3) Concerns over possibility of fraud in E-commerce (such as issues of confidence and trust) and (4) Implementing prescriptions for recovery and growth taking in to consideration the development agenda and unique circumstances of individual country.

STRATEGIC HRM AS A RESPONSE TO THE CHALLENGES OF GLOBALISATION

Strategic Human Resource Management (SHRM) involve a set of internally consistent policies and practices designed and implemented to ensure that a firm's human capital (employees) contribute to the achievement of its business objectives (Baird and Meshoulam, 1988; Delery and Doty, 1996; Huselid, et al., 1997; Jackson and 4 Schuler, 1995). Schuler (1992: 18) has developed a more comprehensive academic definition of SHRM:

> Strategic human resources management is largely about integration and adaptation. Its concern is to ensure that: (1) human resources management (HRM) is fully integrated with the strategy and the strategic needs of the firm; (2) HRM policies cohere both across policy areas and across hierarchies; and (3) HR practices are adjusted, accepted, and used by line managers and employees as part of their everyday work.

> For Wright and McMahan (1992), SHRM refers to "the pattern of planned human resource deployments and activities intended to enable an organisation to achieve its goals" (p. 298). To sum up, it appears that some of the frequently cited fundamental elements of SHRM in the literature are: SHRM practices are macro-oriented, proactive and long term focussed in nature; views human resources as assets or investments not expenses; implementation of SHRM practices bears linkage to organisational performance; and focussing on the alignment of human resources with firm strategy as a means of gaining competitive advantage (Nee and Khatri, 1999:311).

THEORETICAL FOUNDATIONS OF STRATEGIC HRM THEORY

Several theoretical perspectives have been developed to organise knowledge of how HR practices are impacted by strategic considerations as briefly described below. Wright and McMahan (1992) have developed a comprehensive theoretical framework consisting of six theoretical influences. Four of these influences provide explanations for practices resulting from strategy considerations. These include, among others, the resource-based view of the firm and behavioural view. The two other 5 theories provide explanations for HR practices that are not driven by strategy considerations: (1) Resource Dependence and (1) Institutional Theory.

The *resource-based theory of the firm* blends concepts from organisational economics and strategic management (Barney, 1991). This theory holds that a firm's resources are key determinants of its competitive advantage. Firms can develop this competitive advantage only by creating value in a way that is difficult for competitors to imitate. Traditional sources of competitive advantage such as financial and natural resources, technology and economies of scale can be used to create value. However, the resource-based argument is that these sources are increasingly accessible and easy to imitate. Thus they are less significant for competitive advantage especially in comparison to a complex social structure such as an employment system. If that is so, human resource policies and practices may be an especially important source of sustained competitive advantage (Jackson and Schuler, 1995; Pfeffer, 1994). Specifically, four empirical indicators of the potential of firm resources to generate competitive advantage are: value, rareness, imitability and substitutability (Barney (1991). In other words, to gain competitive advantage, the resources available to competing firms must be variable among competitors and these resources must be rare (not easily obtained). Three types of resources associated with organisations are: (a) physical (plant, technology and equipment, geographic location); (b) human (employees' experience and knowledge); and (c) organisational (structure, systems for planning, monitoring, and controlling activities; social relations within the organisation and between the organisation and external constituencies). HR practices greatly influence an organisation's human and organisational resources and so can be used to gain competitive advantages (Schuler and MacMillan, 1984)

The second theoretical influence is the *behavioural view* based on contingency theory. This view explains practices designed to control and influence attitudes and 6 behaviours, and stresses the instrumentality of such practices in achieving strategic objectives. The *cybernetic system* explains the adoption or abandonment of HR practices resulting from feedback on contributions to strategy. For example, training programmes may be adopted to help pursue a strategy and would be subsequently adopted or abandoned based on feedback. The fourth influence, based on *transaction costs* explains why organisations use control systems such as performance evaluation and reward systems. The argument is that in the absence of performance evaluation systems linked to reward systems, strategies might not be pursued. The other two theories provide explanations for HR practices that are not driven by strategy considerations but based on power and political influences, control of resources *(resource-based theory)* and expectations of social responsibility *(institutional theory)* (Greer, 1995: 107-8).

IMPLICATIONS FOR HRM PRACTICES

The idea that individual HR practices impacts on performance in an additive fashion (Delery and Doty, 1996) is inconsistent with the emphasis on internal fit in the resource-based view of the firm. With its implicit systems perspective, the resource based view suggests the importance of "complementary resources", the notion that individual policies or practices "have limited ability to generate competitive advantage" (Barney, 1995:56). This idea, that a system of HR practices may be more than the sum of the parts, appears to be consistent with discussions of synergy, configurations, contingency factors, external and internal fit, holistic approach, etc (Delery and Doty, 1996; Huselid, 1995). Drawing on the theoretical works of Osterman (1987), Sonnenfeld and Peiperl (1988), Kerr and Slocum (1987) and Miles and Snow (1984), Delery and Doty (1996) identified seven practices that are consistently considered strategic HR practices. These are: (1) internal career opportunity; (2) formal training systems; (3) appraisal measures; (4) profit sharing; (5) employment security; (6) voice mechanisms; and (7) job definition. There are other SHRM practices that might affect organisational performance. For example, Schuler and Jackson (1987) presented a very comprehensive list of HR practices. However, the seven practices listed by Delery and Doty above appear to have the greatest support across a diverse literature.

An obvious question at this juncture is: How can organisations effectively adopt, implement and maximise HRM practices for valued firm level outcomes? That is, how can firms increase the probability that they will adopt and then effectively implement appropriate HRM practices? Insuring that members of the HRM personnel have the appropriate human capital or competencies has been suggested as one way to increase the likelihood of effective implementation of HRM practices (Huselid, et al., 1997).

Ulrich and Yeung (1989) argue that the future HR professional will need four basic competencies to become partners in the strategic management process. These include business competence, professional and technical knowledge, integration competence and ability to manage change.

On the other hand, the United Kingdom-based Management Charter Initiative (MCI), an independent competence-based management development organisation, identifies seven key roles and required competencies. These include competencies required to manage roles like managing activities, managing resources, managing people, managing information, managing energy, managing quality and managing projects (MCI Management Standards, April, 1997). Finally, Huselid, et al (1997) identified two sets of HR personnel competencies as important for HR personnel: (1) HR professional competencies; and (2) Business-related competencies.

HR professional competence describes the state-of-the-art HR knowledge, expertise and skill relevant for performing excellently within a traditional HR functional department such as recruitment and selection, training, compensation, etc. This competence insures that technical HR knowledge is both present and used within a firm (Huselid, et al., 1997). *Business-related competence* refers to the amount of business experience HR personnel have had outside the functional HR specialty. These capabilities should facilitate the selection and implementation of HRM policies and practices that fit the unique characteristics of a firm including its size, strategy, structure, and culture (Jackson and Schuler, 1995). In other words, these competencies will enable the HR staff to know the company's business and understand its economic and financial capabilities necessary for making logical decisions that support the company's strategic plan based on the most accurate information possible.

HRM AND ORGANISATIONAL PERFORMANCE

Researchers in SHRM posit that greater use of such practices will always result in better (or worse) organisational performance (Abowd, 1990; Gerhart and Milkovich, 1990; Huselid, 1995; Leonard, 1990; Terpstra and Rozell, 1993). Leonard (1990) found that organisations having long-term incentive plans for their executives had larger increases in return on equity over a four-year period than did other organisations. Abowd (1990) found that the degree to which managerial compensation was based on an organisation's financial performance was significantly related to future financial performance. Gerhart and Milkovich (1990) found that pay mix was related to financial performance. Organisations with pay plans that included a greater amount of performance contingent pay achieved superior financial performance. In combination, these studies indicate that organisations with stronger pay-for-performance norms achieved better long-term financial performance than did organisations with weaker pay-for-performance norms.

Terpstra and Rozell (1993) posited five "best" staffing practices and found that the use of these practices had a moderate and positive relationship with organisational performance. Finally, Huselid (1995) identified a link between organisation-level outcomes and groups of high performance work practices. Instead of focussing on a single practice (e.g., staffing), Huselid assessed the simultaneous use of multiple sophisticated HR practices and concluded that the HR sophistication of an organisation was significantly related to turnover, organisational productivity and financial performance.

In the case of requisite competencies for HR personnel, emerging evidence from empirical research demonstrates the increasing need for HR personnel to have both HR professional and business-related skills and competencies. A survey of HR executives in the US show that HR managers are spending relatively less time in record keeping and auditing, while their time spent in their activities as a business partner have doubled. The survey also revealed that HR managers believe that their HR staffs most important skill needs are team skills, consultation skills and an understanding of business (Noe, et al., 1997).

Managerial competencies particularly in the HR function bring two advantages to the HR function: (1) Enhance the status of the HR department (Barney and Wright, 1988); (2) Act as important influences on the level of integration between HR management and organisation strategy (Golden and Ramanujam, 1985; Ropo, 1993). A study of Singaporean companies found that when HR managers lack the necessary skills to perform their duties competently, line managers and executives take over some of the functions of HR managers (Nee and Khatri, 1999). Research on managerial competencies by Ropo (1993:51) stressed "the internal dynamism of the HR function serves as the most critical mechanism to keep the integration process going after it has been started under favourable organisational and strategic circumstances". Other studies show that if HR managers can evaluate their priorities and acquire new sets of professional and personal competencies, the HR function would be able to ride the wave of business evolution proudly with other functions in the organisation (Becker and Gerhart, 1996; Ulrich, et al., 1995).

Huselid, et al (1997) conducted an elaborate study on 293 firms in the US to evaluate the impact of human resource managers' professional/technical competencies on HR practices and the latter's impact on organisational performance. Results of the study suggest that consistent with the resource-based view of the firm, there exist a significant relationship between SHRM practices and firm performance. They found that: (1) HR related competencies and, to a lesser extent, business-related competencies increase the extent of effective implementation of SHRM practices; and (2) consistent with recent studies linking HRM activities and firm performance (Arthur, 1994; Cutcher-Gershenfeld, 1991; Huselid, 1995; Huselid and Becker, 1996; MacDuffie, 1995), the study support the argument that investments in human resources are a potential source of competitive advantage.

Recent reviews of theoretical and empirical literature (Juhary Ali and Bawa, 1999; Irwin, et al., 1998; Jackson and Schuler, 1995) suggest that a variety of factors affect the relationship between HRM and firm performance. These factors include firm size, technology and union coverage.

HRM practices is fully documented in theoretical and empirical studies. For example, institutional theory suggests that larger organisations should adopt more sophisticated and socially responsive HRM practices because they are more visible and are under more pressure to gain legitimacy. Many empirical studies show that firm size is an important variable influencing HRM practices (Ng and Maki, 1993; Wagar, 1998). There are emerging evidences that HR practices may differ in organisations depending on the *level of technological sophistication* in terms of training (Majchrzak, 1988), performance appraisal (Ouchi, 1977, 1980; Snell, 1992) and reward systems (Kaus, 1990; Snell and Dean, 1992).

Theoretical and empirical studies also support the position that the presence of specific HRM practices may differ based on the union *coverage* of a firm (Ng and Maki, 1993, Wagar, 1998; Lawler and Mohrman 1987).

FRAMEWORK AND PROPOSITIONS

From the discussions so far, the following issues emerge: (1) That there appears to be a significant relationship between strategic HRM practices and firm performance (low employee turnover, high productivity and high profitability (Huselid, et al., 1997);(2) It is also clear that there exist low incidence of implementing SHRM practices relative to technical HRM practices (Huselid, et al., 1997; Wright and McMahan, 1992); (3) Further more although there exists a significant relationship between the extent of both HR professional and business-related managerial competencies and the incidence of implementing HRM practices, organisations have achieved higher levels of HR professional competencies relative to business-related competencies; (4) Finally, environmental context variables like firm size, technology and union status affect the extent of implementing HRM practices (Jackson and Schuler, 1995; Snell and Dean, 1992; Wagar, 1998). The relationships discussed above are presented in the figure below and relevant propositions derived. This theoretical framework is in keeping with the thinking of a number of authors including Delery and Doty (1996), Huselid, et al. (1997), Jackson and Schuler (1995) and Wright and McMahan (1992).

The following testable propositions are derived from the framework for Human Resource Management. (*See box item on next page*)

1. Human resource managers may have achieved higher levels of HR professional competencies and lower levels of business related competencies;

2. The incidence of implementing strategic HR practices is lower in organisations especially in the developing countries;

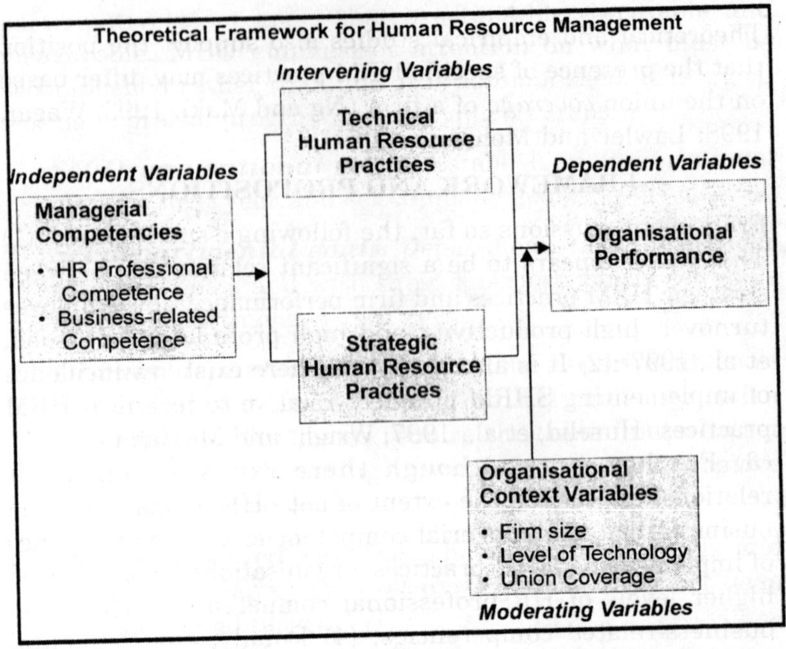

3. Both HR professional competence and knowledge of the business (business related competence) significantly contribute to the extent of implementing SHRM Practices;
4. Managerial competencies are significantly related to organisational performance;
5. The extent of implementing SHRM practices contribute significantly to firm level outcomes;
6. The relationship between SHRM and organisational performance is affected by organisational context variables (firm size, level of technology and union coverage).

It may be pertinent to point out here that the six propositions derived from the framework are particularly relevant for giving insights into the HRM challenges facing organisations in the new era globalisation. In other words, these propositions will help us organise thought on the level of readiness (and otherwise) of organisations in response to the challenges of the global business environment. For example, if HR personnel especially in developing countries demonstrates higher levels of HR professional competence relative to the business-related competence (as found in the literature), it would be important to set right this wrong as a stepping stone for succeeding in global business. This is because to succeed in the new era of globalisation, the human factor is central. That is why it is necessary for HR personnel to prove themselves beyond reasonable doubt that they are capable of playing key roles in enhancing the status of the HR department (Barney and Wright, 1988), must possess a thorough understanding of business (Noe, et al., 1997) and also act as important influences in the level of integration between HR management and organisational strategy (Golden and Ramanujam, 1985; Ropo, 1993).

CONCLUSIONS

This paper set out as a contribution to the current discourse on the interaction of globalisation and business performance especially with a flavour of the challenges from the perspectives of developing countries such as Malaysia and Nigeria. This paper presents a framework for Strategic Human Resource Management as a response to prepare organisations for the challenges of globalisation. It has been observed that by and large organisations have achieved relatively low levels of effectiveness in implementing Strategic Human Resource Management (SHRM) practices (Huselid, et al., 1997). If the propositions outlined above are supported, then the real challenge for organisations in the era of globalisation is to pay particular emphasis to strengthening their human resources by upgrading the relevant competencies.

As governments and corporate bodies brace up for the new millennium characterised by an ever-increasing global challenge, developing countries have no choice but to develop and continuously upgrade the human resource and business competencies of their workforce. In the case of developing countries, distinct competencies are important to deal with not only the HR issues but also others including partnerships in economic recovery especially in South East Asia, dealing with the "big boys", the fund managers, concerns over possibility of fraud in E-commerce with fast spread of Information Technology and last but not least, implementing prescriptions for recovery and growth taking in to consideration the development agenda and unique circumstances of individual countries. Addressing these issues is a necessary step towards facing the challenges of globalisation in to the next millennium.

REFERENCES

Abowd, J.M. 1990. Does Performance-based Compensation Affect Corporate Performance? *Industrial and Labour Relations Review,* 43: 52-73.

Arthur, J.B. 1994. Effects of Human Resource Systems on Manufacturing Performance and Turnover. *Academy of Management Journal,* 37: 670-687.

Barney, J. 1991. Firm Resources and Sustained Competitive Advantage. *Journal of Management,* 17:99-120.

Barney, J.B. and Wright, P.M. 1988. On Becoming a Strategic Partner: The Role of Human Resources in Gaining Competitive Advantage. *Human Resource Management,* 37(1):31-46.

Baird, L and Meshoulam, I. 1988. Managing the Two Fits of Strategic Human Resource Management. *Academy of Management Review,* 13:116-28.

Cutcher-Gershenfeld, J. 1991. The Impact on Economic Performance of a Transformation in Workplace Relations. *Industrial and Labour Relations Review,* 44:241-60.

Delery, J.E. and Doty, D.H. 1996. Modes of Theorising in Strategic Human Resource Management: Tests of Universalistic, Contingency and Configurational Performance Predictions. *Academy of Management Journal,* 39(4): 802-835.

Dowling, P.J., Schuler, R.S. and Welch, D.E. 1994. *International Dimensions of Human Resource Management.* Belmont, CA: Wadsworth.

Gerhart, B. and Milkovich, G.T. 1990. Organisational Differences in Managerial Compensation and Financial Performance. *Academy of Management Journal,* 33: 663-91.

Golden, K.A. and Ramanujam, V. 1985. Between a Dream and a Nightmare: On the Integration of Human Resource Management and Strategic Business Planning. *Human Resource Management,* 24(4): 429-452.

Greer, C.R. 1995. *Strategy and Human Resources: A General Managerial* Perspective. Englewood Cliffs, New Jersey: Prentice Hall.

Hassan, S.M.J. 1992. Human Resource Management in a New Era of Globalism. *Business Forum* 17(1), Los Angeles, Winter: 56-66.

Huselid, M.A., Jackson, S.E. and Randall, R.S. 1997. Technical and Strategic Human Resource Management Effectiveness as Determinants of Firm Performance. *Academy of Management Journal,* 40(1):171-188.

3

Quality Management and Employee Performance in TQM

Rabi Narayan Misra♣
Satyabrata Dash♠

INTRODUCTION

This study provides evidence of the relationship between total quality management (TQM) practices and human resource management (HRM) functions i.e. performance appraisal by documenting those criteria of a performance appraisal system that is congruent with quality precepts. The congruity between performance appraisal criteria and TQM precepts is used as a proxy for employees' positive attitudes towards effective TQM implementation. In a TQM context, as stated by Ghorpade et al., (1995) "the system that is used to appraise performance needs to be congruent with the culture and principles that guide the conduct of the organisation. Unless congruence is retained, anything that is developed is liable to be rejected." Therefore, the current study aims to explain

♣ Dr. Rabi Narayan Misra, Professor, P.G. Centre for Management Studies, S.M.I.T., Berhampur, India.

♠ Dr. Satyabrata Dash,Lecturer, P.G. Centre for Management Studies, S.M.I.T., Berhampur, India.

the main difficulties with the topic of performance evaluation through the frame of the quality perspective, and to identify those criteria for improving quality-driven performance appraisal systems which are congruent with the demands of a total quality environment as well as customers' (internal and external) needs and expectations.

Two main issues motivate this study. The first is the controversy between the popularity of TQM and the criticisms about TQM's ability in realising and understanding employee's needs and wants, and its high rate of failure in practice. The past decade has witnessed a remarkable awareness of and growth in TQM practices. Hendricks and Singhal (1996) argue that many organisations are becoming proactive in supporting TQM by recognising firms that have done an outstanding job in implementing TQM through quality awards. However, despite the widespread popularity of TQM, there is considerable skepticism about its value creation potential. Although this article report management and researchers perceptions about incompatibility between TQM practices and other management subsystems, they rarely provide objective data and empirical evidence on TQM failures to support their claims. This study is also motivated by the need to set realistic criteria for other management subsystem regarding human factor (i.e. performance appraisal) to be congruent with quality precepts. In this regard, existing empirical research on both quality and performance appraisal issues support this view. TQM researchers identified and claimed that successful implementation of various TQM practices are positively related to HRM functions (Wagner, 1998; Sinclair and Zairi, 1995). HRM encompasses a variety of functions designed to manage, support and develop employee working in organisations. Accordingly, Waldman (1994) argues that quality practices in the area of HRM include a systematic and careful approach to recruitment, the use of teamwork and group problem solving, egalitarian work structures, commitment to training, performance and reward systems. However, some commentators have suggested that quality management faces its biggest problem in 'soft' areas such as workforce management (see, for example, Wilkinson, 1994). A new report from the authoritative Institute for Employment Studies claims that many performance appraisal systems are failing both employees and organisations, and having limited impact on business performance (Cummings, 2001). More importantly, many of recent empirical studies in the HRM literature into the interaction between personnel management issues and quality management have focuses on practices which improve quality performance through other HRM functions. According to Fynes (1999), the absence of HRM practices in TQM environment can significantly undermine a quality involvement programme.

Evidence on the compatibility of performance appraisal system with those of TQM criteria in a quality-driven context can shed light on the value of human factor in successful implementation of quality practices. Examining the works of the researchers of the quality movement (Deming, 1986), clearly indicate that all of them recognise the importance of performance appraisal in a quality driven context. Indeed, Deming is the only one within this group who has given specific and extensive attention to this issue. Deming has made reform of the performance appraisal system as an integral part of his action plan. However, he lists 'evaluation of performance, merit rating and annual review' as the third of his 'Seven Deadly Diseases'. Furthermore, Deming (1986) holds performance appraisal practices of American industry to be a root cause of its quality problems. Despite these tensions, there is still little empirical research conducted in quality management aimed at shedding light on the following questions:

1. Why is performance appraisal, which often justifies a wide range of human decisions in the organisation, on Deming's list of things not to do?
2. What are the key criteria of a quality-driven performance evaluation?

3. To what extent, the current performance appraisal criteria are in line with TQM demands and expectations?
4. How important are these criteria from management and employees' perspectives?

Listed below are some assumptions that serve as a starting point for the study. These assumptions were derived from the research findings of quality gurus and researchers (Cardy, 1998):

- Quality-focussed organisations possess a set of performance criteria compatible with TQM context for measurement of employee performance;
- In a quality-driven context, the system that is used to evaluate performance needs to be congruent with the culture and principles that guide the conduct of the organisation;
- The congruity between TQM precepts and performance appraisal measures is positively associated with acceptance and effective TQM implementation, employee satisfaction, and as a result maximisation of the customer satisfaction. This paper investigates the first two questions by examining the existing literature on TQM and performance evaluation in order to establish the context for the empirical research (questions 3 and 4) and its projected significance within the existing body of literature.

TQM

TQM was born more than two decades ago with the core ideas of W. Edward Deming, Joseph Juran, Philip Crosby and Kaoru Ishikawa. Since then it has become an all-pervasive management philosophy finding its way into most sectors of today's business society (Sousa, 2000). An historical examination of the philosophy and practice of quality reveals that TQM encompasses a vast spectrum of topics and approaches which is beyond the scope of this section. The focus here will be on major characteristics of the quality approach and similarities in philosophy and practices. The quality precepts and concepts have been summarised and characterised by a number of researchers (see, for example, Black, 1993; Zairi and Youssef, 1995; Powell, 1995; Oakland, 1998; Cardy, 1998).

Taken together, many of quality researchers seem to suggest the following elements to be key to the TQM philosophy:

- ❖ Customer orientation;
- ❖ Prevention approach to errors.

Cardy (1998) argues that customer satisfaction and improvement of customer satisfaction are the central reasons for the practices associated with the quality approach. According to Cardy, customers of a product or service can be either internal or external to the organisation, and the customers are the focus of the quality process and determine the standards and directions for improving performance. The study by Thiagarajan and Zairi in 1997 indicates that the success of implementing TQM in an organisation is ultimately judged by its customers. Therefore, TQM initiative is considered a failure if it fails to optimise operations to continuously add value for customer satisfaction. Similarly, Scholtes (1993) surveyed the TQM literature and identified that "the customers and their needs shape the organisation and its work, not vice versa."

According to the various studies on TQM, another important aspect of the quality approach is an emphasis on prevention rather than detection of errors (see, for example, Deming 1986, 1993; Walton, 1986; Oakland 1998; Cardy 1998). The study by Cardy (1998) indicates traditional Western approach to quality emphasises the post hoc inspection process as a mechanism for ensuring adequate quality. However, Cardy points out that emphasis in TQM approach is on making inspection an integral part of the work process, rather than a separate function that occurs later. Deming (1986), one of the most notable quality advocates, explicitly identified disadvantages to the traditional error detection system. According to Cardy (1998), one disadvantage is that not all defective products or inadequate service interactions can be identified by a separate review function. Additionally, the study by Cardy cautioned that the disadvantage might result in disgruntled customers and decreased demand for the organisation's product or service. Furthermore, there are also direct costs in the production of errors due to the time and cost of material associated with the creation of the defective product or inadequate service interaction. More specifically, Deming (1986) argued that the most important costs of the detection system are the indirect cost. The indirect costs asserted by Deming to be associated with the detection approach include fear and loss of pride in workmanship.

There is considerable support for this argument. Ghorpade et al. (1995) stress that pride in workmanship is a core value of the American workforce. Furthermore, there is also a persistent complaint that this energy is not being harnessed by the corporate sector. The post hoc evaluation by independent inspectors means that errors unrecognised and possibly not produced by the worker can be found and the worker may be held responsible for those outcomes.

In the study of Cardy and his associates (1995) they assert that "the quality approach emphasises the importance of striving to avoid committing errors in the first place." Moreover, workers are given the tools and responsibility for assessing the quality of their own work. As such, quality approach decentralises the traditional inspection function and integrate it into the work process itself. The assumption that errors are largely due to system factors rather than worker characteristics is another important characteristic of the quality approach. Additionally, Cardy (1998) argues that since system factors are assumed to be the major determinant of performance variability, this assumption can be thought of as underlying the prevention emphasis. Specifically, if errors are to be avoided, the most important means for doing this is a focus on the system, not on individual workers. In sum, Cardy states that "performance is mainly a function of system factors and improvement in this performance thus requires improvement in the system."

QUALITY MANAGEMENT AND HRM

Many researchers and quality experts agree that a fundamental assumption of the quality approach is that system factors matter the most when it comes to performance. According to Cardy (1998), system factors refer to anything outside of individual workers. A number of researchers associated with the TQM movement have been highly critical of western performance management practices (Juran, 1989). As noted by Waldman (1994), among these, perhaps the one most strident in his claims has been Deming. Deming (1986) summarised his management philosophy with 14 management principles that he offered as requirements to remain competitive in providing products and services. Deming develops two primary themes relevant to total quality and HRM practices i.e. performance evaluation. The first theme is that the central problem of management is an incorrect understanding of variation in performance phenomena, including the work performance of employees.

Waldman (1994) who attempted to design performance management system for TQM implementation argues that "Deming's lamentation focuses on the confusion between common and special causes of variation." Special causes are sporadic in nature, and with regard to work performance, can include factors unique to the individual worker, i.e. separate from the system in which the individual operates. The sporadic nature of special causes is evident in Deming's proposal that very little of the variance in work performance is due to such causes. In contrast, Waldman notes that the lion's share of variance is due to common causes, which according to Deming are system-based. Cardy (1998), for instance, presents a list of general categories of system factors that could influence performance as follows:

- ❖ Poor coordination of work activities with others;
- ❖ Inadequate information, instructions, specifications, and so on;
- ❖ Lack of needed equipment;
- ❖ Inability to obtain raw materials, parts, supplies, and so on;
- ❖ Inadequate financial resources;
- ❖ Uncooperative co-workers or poor interpersonal relations;
- ❖ Inadequate training insufficient time to produce the quantity or quality of work required of the job;
- ❖ Poor environmental conditions (for example, too cold, hot, noisy, or full of interruptions);
- ❖ Unexpected equipment breakdown.

As noted by Waldman (1994). one of the Deming's main concerns is that management, through such mechanisms as performance appraisal, attempts to respond to most variation as if it were due to special causes rather than to common causes. Further, Deming (1986) argued that system factors account for up to 95 per cent of the variance in performance. However, Cardy (1998) notes that this figure was simply an assertion based on no empirical evidence. Nonetheless, it is a figure routinely cited in the quality literature.

As a result of the above arguments, TQM proponents have been quick to criticise performance evaluation practices which are based on the assumption that the individual employee is largely in control of his or her own performance level (Deming, 1986; Scherkenbach, 1985; Scholtes, 1993; Walton, 1986). It follows that a second primary theme of total quality is that a process (or work performance in a unit) can only be improved by first identifying and eliminating the special causes of variation to achieve a stable process. Then the overall system can be improved by focussing attention on the common, system-based factors which affect performance. As stated by Cardy (1998), "underlying the focus on system improvement is the quality assumption that people are intrinsically motivated to perform well." In other words, the emphasis from the quality perspective is on removing system barriers to performance in order to provide an opportunity for the natural motivation of workers to be released. However, this argument appears to be in sharp contrast to the approach taken by traditional HRM. HRM theory and practice have for many years focussed on individual differences in the management of performance in organisations. Indeed, areas such as selection, performance appraisal, and compensation have largely been concerned with decision-making based on assessment of individual differences. An underlying assumption by traditional HRM has been that individuals matter in the determination of work performance variation. According to the study by Cardy (1998), "systematic examination of job is important in HRM so that individual differences important to the job can be identified, measured and trained." Thus, individual differences such as knowledge, skills, and abilities of workers are believed to be important and direct determinants of performance. Furthermore, the HRM field has assumed that worker motivation is largely determined by extrinsic factors. While intrinsic motivation has sporadically been recognised as potentially important, thrust has been on setting extrinsic contingencies to maximise performance. Examples of the extrinsic motivation approach taken by HRM are `clear and difficult performance goals' and 'performance-contingent pay'. However, Proponents of TQM have questioned this focus, and instead have chosen to emphasise aspects of work systems as being predominantly relevant to work performance (see, for example, Deming, 1986,1993; Juran, 1989; Walton, 1986; Cardy, 1998). Cardy (1998) conducted a comprehensive review of literature pertaining to performance evaluation in quality organisational environments and concluded that "there is a clearly fundamental conflict between the quality and traditional HRM."

PERFORMANCE EVALUATION

Recent years have seen the evolvement of performance appraisal systems and human resource development processes. More importantly, in comparison to other HRM functions survey data indicates that increasing attention is being paid to employee appraisal. Storey (1995) argues that in comparison to recruitment and selection, there have been more systematic, longitudinal surveys on its use. While the traditional name, performance appraisal is still in use, some organisations are seeing negatives connotations with the term. For many, the term 'performance appraisal system' embodies the major difficulties with traditional approaches. A review of the literature on performance appraisal reveals the main difficulties with traditional performance appraisal systems as follows:

- A focus on the past;
- Use of quantifiable measures;
- Traits are inputs to work, not outputs;
- Traits are subjective;
- Conservative use of performance appraisal rating scale;
- Pay awards 'unrelated' to performance appraisal;
- Annual performance appraisal emphasising formal procedures;
- The limits of only two performance appraisal views;
- Performance appraisal forms can impeding wider discussion;
- Performance appraisal objectives are not always measurable;
- Different performance appraisal schemes for different employees.

Thus, the purpose of traditional performance appraisal systems was largely to ensure that the minimum standards for the job were being maintained and that some measure of control was being exerted over the employee. This was referred to as 'Performance Control' by Randell (1994). In general, the performance appraisal attempted to assess past and current performance in a particular job. These were often viewed as an opportunity to criticise rather than give recognition or meaningful support for performance improvement. These performance appraisal processes may or may not have included performance related pay increases. These traditional performance appraisal systems tended not to incorporate corporate goals and the direction or strategic needs of the business, or the personal aspirations of employees and their future development.* In contrast, during recent years performance appraisal systems have tended to move away from being primarily control and maintenance based and have moved towards an approach more concerned with motivational and developmental issues to be congruent with the culture and principles that guide the conduct of the organisations. In case of a TQM context, for example, the performance appraisal focus should become one of the linking corporate strategic objectives with an employees' personal aspirations and developmental needs and continually reviewing, developing and improving their performance and potential. The major shifts in recent years in performance appraisal have been to:

- Focus the appraisal on development rather than control;
- Use open consensus based approaches;
- Assess performance against behavioural standards and competencies;
- Draw performance feedback from colleagues and subordinates;

---

* Performance Appraisal: A UK Based Company (No date), Performance Appraisal Systems, Traditional and Recent Performance Appraisal [Online]. Available: http://www.performanceappraisal.co.uk/index.htm. [Access: February 2001].

- ❖ Relate the appraisal results to performance related pay schemes;
- ❖ Minimise paperwork while increasing ownership of the process;
- ❖ Focus the process on people's potential rather than skills deficits.

In addition to these major shifts in performance evaluation, Ghorpade et al. (1995) point out that "performance appraisal is a complex creativity that confronts even the most well-meaning appraiser with a maze of interrelations that frustrate assignment of clean, accurate, and merit-based ratings." Moreover, they argue that appraisal gets progressively more complicated with the introduction of additional variables and quality demands. Even modest increments in complexity add disproportionately to the challenge. According to them, as complexity increases, it becomes progressively more difficult to meet the criteria that good appraisal systems need to meet i.e. observability, measurability, job relatedness, importance to job success, controlability, and practicality.

TQM AND PERFORMANCE EVALUATION

Employee or staff appraisal can be defined as the process whereby current performance in a job is observed and discussed for the purpose of adding to that level of performance (Randell, 1994). Even though this is a simple definition of an every day managerial activity it is a controversial topic. The literature abounds with different analyses and conclusions that arise from how the process of employee performance measurement is viewed and how it is seen to fit with business strategy, personnel policy and individual managerial philosophies. A brief review of the literature indicates that performance appraisal has been lamented by many researchers as an unwelcome and difficult task for a variety of reasons i.e. a tool for managerial control, focus on the past, individual responsibility for performance, error and bias. Even though the role of evaluation may be uncomfortable for many, Cardy (1998) asserts that 'judgments of performance are needed if performance contingent decisions, ranging from termination to pay increase and promotion, are to have any sort of rational basis.' The remainder of this section examines the conflicts between traditional and quality approaches to performance appraisal in order to find out the characteristics of performance appraisal that could maximise the effectiveness of appraisal in a quality-driven context. Most advocates of total quality believe that TQM and performance appraisal are incompatible. For them, company managers can choose to promote either of these approaches but not both. In an attempt to explain the fundamental problems with performance evaluation in quality-focussed organisations, Scholtes (1993) argues that since fundamental TQM requirements contradict the basic elements of performance appraisal, it would be impossible to combine them. However, in a recent study of high performance organisations the practice of employing a value-added performance appraisal process was cited as one of top ten vehicles for creative competitive advantage (Longenecker and Fink, 1999). In a similar study, Shadur et al. (1994) found that most large organisations surveyed have some form of performance appraisal and they provided evidence supporting the positive effects of performance appraisal on productivity and quality. Furthermore, according to Baird and Meshoulam (1988), a firm's HRM activities must fit with each other and support other management programmes if peak organisational performance is to be achieved. Supporting the HR practices and internal fit viewpoints, Arthur (1994) concluded that "HR practices focussed on enhancing employee commitment, were related to higher performance." In addition, Sinclair and Zairi (1995) examined the performance measurement in quality-focussed organisations and found that an inappropriate performance measurement could be a major cause of failure in the implementation of TQM. A survey conducted at the European Centre for TQM has revealed that even in companies assumed to be leaders in both performance measurement and TQM, a significant gap exists between the aspects of performance, which managers perceive as being important to measure, and the actual performance measures used. Consequently, this prevents the organisations from optimising, meaning that all components of the system are not working together. Although opinions vary on how best to correct the problem, the remainder of this section focuses on the main disadvantages of the current performance evaluation systems in TQM-based organisations in order to identify the key generic criteria of a quality-driven performance appraisal. Therefore, the consistency between TQM practices and performance appraisal criteria is a critical principle if TQM practices are to remain acceptable and successful throughout the organisation. As mentioned earlier, many teachers of total quality, following the lead of W. Edwards Deming, suggest that TQM and performance evaluation are incompatible. Indeed. Deming lists 'evaluation of performance, merit rating and annual review' as the third of his 'seven deadly diseases'. Even though Deming has not enumerated his criticisms, Gho rpade et al. (1995) note that the following four charges keep recurring in his discussion:

1. Current performance appraisal practices are unfair since they hold the worker responsible for errors that may be the result of faults within the system;
2. Current performance appraisal practices promote worker behaviour that compromises quality;
3. Current performance appraisal practices create a band of discouraged workers who cease trying to excel;
4. Current performance appraisal practices rob the workers of their pride in workmanship.

Similarly, Scholtes (1993) points out that there are principles at the heart of the quality that establish a foundation for the new philosophy and, indirectly, the basis for rejecting employee performance measurement. More importantly, according to Scholtes, in the era of TQM, performance management supports obsolete values with dysfunctional methods. Specifically, in his view performance evaluation:

- Disregards and, in fact, undermines teamwork;
- Disregards the existence of a system;
- Disregards variability in the system;
- Uses a measurement system that is unreliable and inconsistent;
- Encourages an approach to problem-solving that is superficial and culprit-oriented;
- Tends to establish an aggregate of safe goals in an organisation;
- Creates losers, cynics, and wasted human resources;
- Seeks to provide a means to administer multiple managerial functions (pay, promotion, feedback communication, direction-setting, etc.), yet it is inadequate to accomplish any of them.

In a more accurate language, among other issues, the fundamental problem with performance appraisal from the perspective of many quality advocates is that it holds workers responsible for outcomes that are beyond their control. However, Cardy (1998) reasonably argues that "if performance is largely due to system factors, then it makes little sense to assess the workers, since they contribute such a small amount to the performance outcomes."

In regard to the importance of an effective performance evaluation system, Ghorpade *et al.* (1995) note that appraisal of human performance at work is inevitable in all organisations i.e. large and small, public and private, local and multinational. They identify three main reasons for this:

1. Individuals are hired by organisations to perform work needed for the success of the organisation. So, performance appraisal is the organisation's way of assessing whether it is getting its rightful due from the individual;

2. Individuals differ concerning how well and how conscientiously they do their work. Therefore, appraisal is necessary to account for the differences in contributions of individuals;

3. In today's legal climate, formal performance appraisal is essential to defend the organisation's negative actions against individuals, particularly those that adversely affect members of minority groups protected by law.

In sum, the appraisal and management of performance remains as an important issue in organisations. Even though the role of evaluation may be uncomfortable for many, Cardy (1998) states that "judgments of performance are needed if performance contingent decisions ranging from termination to pay increase and promotion are to have any sort of rational basis." According to Cardy, there is no doubt that the appraisal and management of human performance can be a difficult and error-ridden task. However, it is important to both the organisational and individual perspectives that the task still be done as effectively as possible.

The managerial literature is replete with the ideas of how performance can be appraised at the workplace. However, before examining the rich collection, it is useful to make an observation that is now widely accepted as axiomatic: as Ghorpade *et al.* (1995) put it, "the system that is used to appraise performance needs to be congruent with the culture and principles that guide the conduct of the organisation. Unless congruence is retained, anything that is developed is liable to be rejected." Therefore, what follows are several prescriptions for improving quality-driven performance appraisal systems which are congruent with the demands of a total quality environment. However, these recommendations are fairly generic and may need to be customised and embellished in order to best work in each particular quality environment. The intent of the suggestions is to provide some general direction for maximising the effectiveness of performance appraisal in quality environments. To help quality-driven organisations to decide what criteria are most appropriate for performance measurement, Ghorpade et al. (1995) describe a number of performance measurement criteria compatible with TQM culture in simple and rather prescriptive terms as follows:

- Within a quality environment, the primary purpose of performance appraisal should be to help the employees improve their performance;
- Modification of the existing performance appraisal system should be brought about with the active involvement of all those who are affected by the activity;
- The evaluation of the existing performance appraisal system should be approached like any other quality improvement effort;
- Within a quality-driven environment, the focus of appraisal should be on behaviour, with output and input used for diagnostic and developmental purposes;
- For each dimension of performance considered, employees should be asked to provide examples of two types of behaviour: task performance and quality improvement;
- Workers should be judged by absolute rather than relative standards of performance;
- Responsibility for appraisal should continue to rest with the manager.

Scholtes (1993) in a critique article began to attack on the concepts and practice of performance evaluation, and argues that since fundamental TQM requirements contradict the basic elements of performance evaluation, it would be impossible to combine them. To tackle the problem, Scholtes suggests two alternatives to performance appraisal that he believes managers don't like to hear. First, he believes that "until managers let go of their obsession with the individual worker and understand the importance of systems and processes, they will not enter the quality era." In addition, Scholtes notes that without this change in mind-set, managers will continue to look for alternatives that are no different from what they are trying to replace. Second, Scholtes states that "when managers are doing something that is demonstrably harmful, they can stop doing it without finding an alternative way to harm themselves." Cardy (1998) devotes a chapter of the book 'Performance appraisal: State of the art in practice' to performance appraisal in quality context and say about 'traditional HRM and Quality-Oriented HRM' that "there is a definite and fundamental conflict between traditional HRM and quality. The HRM discipline emphasise a main effect for person factors while the quality approach emphasises a main effect for system factors." Moreover, Cardy argues that it is not that one approach is right and the other wrong.

Rather, either approach alone is deficient.

Content

- Includes assessment of both person and system factors;
- Generates specific descriptions of system factors;
- Take a participative approach to distinguishing between person and system factors;
- Take a behavioural approach to measuring person factors;
- At the individual level, recognise that system factors may be influenced by person characteristics;
- Shift appraisal to a partnership focussed on improving performance rather than placing blame;
- Explore the possibility that differences between rater and ratee assessments of system factors indicate areas of difficulty in the work situation that the rater may not be aware of;

- Watch out for the tendency of ratees to use system factors as excuses, particularly in a climate with low trust;
- Use both person and system factors to allow for the determination and improvement of person fit with the work situation;
- Deal explicitly with causal attribution so that accurate diagnosis of performance can be made and effective remedies be introduced;
- Include sources that are most knowledgeable about the person and system factors that influence the worker's performance;
- Involve both internal and external customers in setting standards and in assessing performance.

CONCLUSION

This paper provides an insight into the issues involved in the development of a quality-driven performance appraisal that complements total quality management. It has contrasted TQM precepts and HRM approaches to employee performance appraisal in the workplace. In particular, the quality contention that appraisal should be eliminated was examined in detail. It was further revealed that for measuring the real contribution of employees into quality programmes certain criteria such as 'focus on behaviour, absolute standard, active involvement of all employees, emphasis on collective responsibility for quality, situational performance factors, a process focus, and customer care are more compatible with TQM context. Only through such quality-focussed will TQM-based organisations create a quality-driven performance by valuation system.

From the literature survey it revealed that performance evaluation is still a vital necessity in quality-driven context, but it needs to be adapted in important ways so that the practice maximally contributes to the quality effort. More importantly, the findings from this survey establish the context for the empirical research and its projected significance within the existing body of the literature.

REFERENCES

1. Adebanjo, D. and Kehoe D. (1999), 'An Investigation of Quality Culture Development in UK Industry', *International Journal of Operation and Production Management,* Vol. 19, No. 7, pp. 633-649.
2. Arthur, J. B. (1994), 'Effects of Human Resource Systems on Manufacturing Performance and Turnover', *Academy of Management Journal.* Vol. 37, pp. 670-687.
3. Baird, L. and Meshoulam I. (1988), 'Managing Two Fits of Strategic Human Resource Management'. *Academy of Management Review,* Vol. 13, pp. 116-128.
4. Black, S.A. (1993), 'Measuring the Critical Factors of Total Quality Management, *Ph.D. Thesis.* University of Bradford.
5. Cardy, R.L. and Dobbins G.H. (1996). 'Human Resource Management in a Total Quality Management Environment: Shifting from a Traditional to a TQHRM Approach'. *Journal of Quality Management,* Vol. I, pp. 5-20.
6. Cardy, R.L. (1998). 'Performance Appraisal in a Quality Context: A New Look at an Old Problem'. In Smither J.W. (ed), *Performance Appraisal: State of the Art in Practice;* San Francisco: Jossey-Bass Publishers.
7. Crosby, P.B. (1979). 'Quality is Free: The Art of Making Quality Certain '. New York: New American Library.
8. Crosby, P.B. (1984). 'Quality Without Tears: The Art of Hassle-free Management, Quality Press, Milwaukee, WI.
9. Cummings N. (2001). 'Staff Appraisal Needs Shake-up': *OR News Letter,* p. 4. May.
10. Deming, W.E. (1986). 'Out of the Crisis'; Cambridge, M.A.: Centre for Advanced Engineering Study. Massachusetts Institute of Technology.
11. Deming, W.E. (1993). 'The New Economics for Industry. Government, Education'. Centre for Advanced Engineering Study, Massachusetts Institute of Technology, Cambridge, MA.
12. Dowerty, W. (1996), 'Assessment and Self-assessment of Total Quality Management in Organisations, Using Knowledge-based Techniques, *Ph.D. Thesis,* Queen's University Belfast.

13. Flynes B. (1999), 'Quality Management Practices: A Review of the Literature', *Irish Business and Administration Research (IBAR),* Vol.19/20. No. 2, pp. 113-138.

14. Fuchsberg, G. (1993), 'Baldrige Award Maybe Losing Some Luster', *Wall Street Journal,* p. B1, April 19.

15. Ghorpade, J., Chen M.M., and Caggiano J. (1995), 'Creating Quality-driven Performance Appraisal Systems', *The Academy of Management Executive,* Vol. 9, No. l, pp. 32-40.

16. Hendricks, K.B. Singhal V.R. (1996) 'Quality Awards and the Market Value of the Firm: An Empirical Investigation', Management Science, Vol: 42 No. 3, pp. 415-436.

17. Ishikawa, K. (1985), 'What is Total Quality Control? The Japanese Way', Englewood Cliffs, NJ: Prentice-Hall Inc.

18. Juran, I.M. (1989). 'Juran on Planning for Quality, New York. NY: The Free Press.

19. Juran, I.M. (1964), 'Managerial Breakthrough', McGraw-Hill, New York.

20. Lewis, D.A. (1992), 'A Comparison of Attitudes of Spanish and American Quality Assurance Managers', *International Journal of Production and Inventory Management;* Vol: 33(1), pp. 42-45.

21. Longenecker, C.O., Fink L. S. (1999) 'Creating Effective Performance Appraisal', *Industrial Management,* Vol. 41, No. 5, pp. 18-21.

22. Oakland, J.S. (1998), *'Total Quality Management: Text with Cases',* 4th ed., McGraw-Hill.

23. Performance Appraisal: A UK Based Company (No date), Performance Appraisal Systems, Traditional and Recent Performance Appraisal [Online]. Available: http://www.performanceappraisal.co.uk/index.htm. [Access: February 2001].

24. Powell Thomas C. (1995); 'Total Quality Management as Competitive Advantage: A Review and Empirical Study', *'Strategic Management Journal,* Vol. 16 No. l, pp. 15-37.

25. Randell G. (1994). 'Employee Appraisal'. In Sisson K. (ed), *'Personnel Management: A Comprehensive Guide to Theory and Practice in Britain';* Oxford: Blackwell Publishers Ltd.

26. Scherkenbach, W.W. (1998). 'Performance Appraisal and Quality: Ford's New Philosophy', *Quality Progress,* pp. 40-46.

27. Scholtes, P.R. (1993) 'Total Quality or Performance Appraisal: Choose One', *National Productivity Review,* Vol. 12, No. 3.

28. Shadur M.A. Rodwell, I.J., Simmons D.E., and Bamber G.J. (1994), 'International Best Practice Quality Management and High Performance: Inferences from the Australian Automotive Sector', *International Journal of Human Resource Management,* Vol. 5 No. 3, pp. 609-631.

29. Sinclair D. and Zairi M. (1995). 'Performance Measurement as an Obstacle to TQM', *The TQM Magazine,* Vol. 7, No. 2, pp. 42-45.

30. Singh, A. (1985) 'TQM: Concept and Practice in India, Productivity, Vol. 32, No. 3, pp. 393-399.

31. Smith, S., Transfield D., Foster M, and Whittle S. (1994), 'Strategies for Managing the TQM Agenda', *International Journal of Operations and Production Management,* Vol. 14. No. l, pp. 75-88.

32. Sousa, R. (2000) 'Quality Management: Universal or Context Dependent? An Empirical Investigation of Customer Focus Practices', *7th International Conference of the European Operations Management Association,* Ghent, Belgium, June 4-7, pp. 564-571.

33. Story John. (1995), 'New Perspectives on Human Resource Management', London: Routledge.

34. Thiagarajan, T, and Zairi M., (1997), 'A Review of Total Quality Management in Practice: Understanding the Fundamentals Through Examples of Best Practice Applications', *The TQM Magazine,* Vol. 9 No. 6, pp. 414-417.

35. Wagner, T.H. (1998), 'Determinants of Human Resource Management Practices in Small Firms: Some Evidence from Atlantic Canada', *Journal of Small Business Management,* Vol. 36, No. 2, pp. 13-23.

36. Waldman David A, (1994),' Designing Management System for Total Quality Implementation', *Journal of Organisational Change Management,* Vol. 7. No. 2, pp. 31-44. MCB University Press.

37. Walton. M. (1986), 'The Deming Management Method'. Pedigree. New York.

38 Wilkinson A, (1994), 'The Other Side of Quality: Soft Issues and the Human Resource Dimension', *Total Quality Management.* Vol. 3, No. 3, pp. 323-329.

39. Zairi M, and Youssef M.A. (1995), 'Benchmarking Critical Factors for TQM, Part 1: Theory and Foundations', *Benchmarking for Quality Management and Technology,* Vol. 2 No. 1. pp. 5-20.

4

Human Resource Management After Globalisation

D. Tata Rao♣
G. Chandrayya♠

INTRODUCTION

The current financial crisis, which has engulfed East Asia since July 1997 and has subsequently spread to Russia and Brazil, is one of the most pressing challenges facing countries and businesses in today's global business environment. Globalisation represents the structural making of the world characterised by the free flow of technology and human resources across national boundaries as well as the spread of Information Technology (IT) and mass media presenting an ever-changing and competitive business environment. Two major limitations are observed in the treatment of the twin issues of the responses to the East Asian economic crisis and the coverage of the literature on globalisation. While the response to the crisis has focussed on macroeconomic aspects,

♣ Dr. D.T. Rao. Department of Commerce, Government Degree College, Yelamanchili, Visakhapatnam District, Andhra Pradesh.

♠ G.Chandrayya, Department of Commerce, Government College (Autonomous), Rajahmundry E.G. District, Andhra Pradesh.

the issue of globalisation has been addressed predominantly in and with respect to the developed economies of Western Europe, North America and Japan. This paper is an attempt to address these two limitations. Since the human factor is the key in the new era of globalisation (Hassan, 1992; Sims and Sims, 1995), the primary objective of this paper is to present a conceptual framework for effective management of human resources as a response to the growing interaction of globalisation and business performance. Three central arguments are made in this paper: (1) That a growing body of evidence converge to suggest that changes taking place in the global business environment often are not accompanied by complementary changes in human resource management practices leading to a situation whereby the failure of some firms is due to the mismanagement of people rather than to problems with technical systems per se; (2) That this is because organisations have achieved relatively low levels effectiveness in implementing Strategic Human Resource Management (SHRM) practices (Huselid, et al., 1997) especially in emerging economies of South East Asia and other developing countries like Nigeria that are exposed to the challenges and opportunities of globalisation; (3) That in order to manage employees for competitive edge in a period of globalisation, human resource personnel must possess competencies relevant for implementing such strategic HRM policies and practices (Barney and Wright, 1988; Huselid, et al., 1997; Ulrich, 1989, 1996; Ulrich, et al., 1995). Guided by theoretical perspectives such as the firm's resource-based theory of competitive advantage (Barney, 1988, 1991; Irwin, et al., 1998; Wright and McMahan, 1992) and empirical evidence (Delery and Doty, 1996; Gittleman, et al., 1998; Huselid, et al., 1997; Leonard, 1990; Pfeffer, 1994; Schuler and Jackson, 1987), this paper develop propositions draws implications for the strategic management of human resources to prepare organisations for the challenges of globalisation.

THE GLOBAL PICTURE

When it comes to business, the world is indeed becoming a smaller place. More and more companies are operating across geographic and cultural boundaries. While most have adapted to the global reality in their operations, many are lagging behind in developing the human resource policies, structures, and services that support globalisation. The human resource function faces many challenges during the globalisation process, including creating a global mind-set within the HR group, creating practices that will be consistently applied in different locations/offices while also maintaining the various local cultures and practices, and communicating a consistent corporate culture across the entire organisation. To meet these challenges, organisations need to consider the HR function not as just an administrative service but as a strategic business partner. Companies should involve the human resources department in developing and implementing both business and people strategies. This type of partnership is necessary if an organisation wants to change potentially inaccurate perceptions of HR and reiterate the HR function's purpose and importance throughout its global environment. Organisations will also discover that HR can be invaluable in facilitating the development of a unifying corporate culture and finding and cultivating much needed leadership talent around the world. The process of globalising resources, both human and otherwise, is challenging for any company. Organisations should realise that their global HR function can help them utilise their existing human talent from across multiple geographic and cultural boundaries. International organisations need to assist and incorporate their HR function to meet the challenges they face if they want to create a truly global workforce. The current financial crisis, which has engulfed East Asia since July 1997 and has subsequently spread to Russia and Brazil, is one of the most pressing challenges facing countries and businesses in todays global business environment. Most of the response to the financial crisis has focussed on macroeconomic aspects and there is relatively little research on the role of human resources. Secondly, the issue of globalisation has been addressed predominantly in, and with respect to, the developed economies of Western Europe, North America and Japan.

This paper is an attempt to address these two limitations since the human factor is one of the key issues in the new era of globalisation (Hassan, 1992; Sims and Sims, 1995). The primary objective of this paper therefore is to present a conceptual framework for strategic management of human resources as a response to the growing interaction of globalisation and business performance.

Three central arguments made in this paper are: (1) That a great deal of evidence has accrued to suggest that changes taking place in the global business environment often are not accompanied by complementary changes in human resource management practices leading to a situation whereby the failure of some firms is due to the mismanagement of people rather than to problems with technical systems per se; (2) That this is because organisations have achieved relatively low levels of effectiveness in implementing Strategic Human Resource Management (SHRM) practices (Huselid, et al., 1997). This is particularly the case in emerging economies of South East Asia like Malaysia and other developing countries like Nigeria that are exposed to the challenges and opportunities of globalisation; (3) That in order to manage employees for competitive edge in a period of globalisation, human resource personnel must possess competencies relevant for effective implementation of such strategic HRM policies and practices (Barney and Wright, 1988; Cunningham and Debrah, 1995; Huselid, et al., 1997; Ulrich, 1987, 1996; Ulrich, et al., 1995). Following Wright and McMahan's (1992) .comprehensive theoretical framework for SHRM, this paper develops competency-based research framework and draws implications for the strategic management of human resources to prepare organisations for the challenges of globalisation.

HRM ISSUES AND CHALLENGES IN GLOBAL MARAKETS

The coming of the 21st century globalisation poses distinctive HRM challenges to businesses especially those operating across national boundaries as multinational or global enterprises.

Global business is characterised by the free flow of human and financial resources especially in the developed economies of European Union (EU), the North American Free Trade Agreement (NAFTA), other regional groupings such as the Association of South East Asian Nations (ASEAN), the Economic Community of West African States (ECOWAS), the Southern African Development Community, etc. These developments are opening up new markets in a way that has never been seen before. This accentuates the need to manage human resources effectively to gain competitive advantage in the global market place. To achieve this, organisations require an understanding of the factors that can determine the effectiveness of various HR practices and approaches. This is because countries differ along a number of dimensions that influence the attractiveness of Direct Foreign Investments in each country. These differences determine the economic viability of building an operation in a foreign country and they have a particularly strong impact on HRM in that operation. A number of factors that affect HRM in global markets are identified: (1) Culture (2) Economic System (3) Political System—the legal framework and (4) Human capital (Noe, et al, 2000: 536). Consistent with the scope of the present paper, only one dimension is treated: human capital (the skills, capabilities or competencies of the workforce). This is in consonance with the believe that competency-based human resource plans provide a source for gaining competitive advantage and for countries profoundly affect a foreign country's desire to locate or enter that country's market (O'Reilly, 1992). This partly explains why Japan and US locate and enter the local markets in South East Asia and Mexico respectively.

In the case of developing countries, globalisation poses distinct challenges to governments, the private sector and organised labour. These challenges, which must be addressed through a strategic approach to human resource management, include—(1) Partnership in economic recovery especially in South East Asia; (2) Dealing with the "big boys", the fund managers; (3) Concerns over possibility of fraud in

E-commerce (such as issues of confidence and trust); and (4) Implementing prescriptions for recovery and growth taking in to consideration the development agenda and unique circumstances of individual country.

The logical question here is what is the appropriate response for businesses in both the developed countries and developing countries like Malaysia and Nigeria to address these imminent challenges? This is the task we take up in the section that follows.

STRATEGIC HRM AS A RESPONSE TO THE CHALLENGES OF GLOBALISATION

Strategic Human Resource Management (SHRM) involve a set of internally consistent policies and practices designed and implemented to ensure that a firm's human capital (employees) contribute to the achievement of its business objectives (Baird and Meshoulam, 1988; Delery and Doty, 1996; Huselid, et al., 1997; 'Jackson and Schuler, 1995). Schuler (1992: 18) has developed a more comprehensive academic definition of SHRM:

Strategic human resources management is largely about integration and adaptation. Its concern is to ensure that: (1) human resources (HR) management is fully integrated with the strategy and the strategic needs of the firm; (2) HR policies cohere both across policy areas and across hierarchies; and (3) HR practices are adjusted, accepted, and used by line managers and employees as part of their everyday work.

Theoretical Foundations of Strategic HRM

Several theoretical perspectives have been developed to organise knowledge of how HR practices are impacted by strategic considerations as briefly described below. Wright and McMahan (1992) have developed a comprehensive theoretical framework consisting of six theoretical influences. Four of these influences provide explanations for practices resulting from strategy considerations. These include, among others, the resource-based view of the firm and behavioural view. The two other theories provide explanations for HR practices that are not driven by strategy considerations: (1) Resource Dependence; and (2) Institutional Theory.

The *resource-based theory of the firm* blends concepts from organisational economics and strategic management (Barney, 1991). This theory holds that a firm's resources are key determinants of its competitive advantage. Firms can develop this competitive advantage only by creating value in a way that is difficult for competitors to imitate. Traditional sources of competitive advantage such as financial and natural resources, technology and economies of scale can be used to create value. However, the resource-based argument is that these sources are increasingly accessible and easy to imitate. Thus they are less significant for competitive advantage especially in comparison to a complex social structure such as an employment system. If that is so, human resource policies and practices may be an especially important source of sustained competitive advantage (Jackson and Schuler, 1995; Pfeffer, 1994).

Specifically, four empirical indicators of the potential of firm resources to generate competitive advantage are: value, rareness, imitability and substitutability (Barney (1991). In other words, to gain competitive advantage, the resources available to competing firms must be variable among competitors and these resources must be rare (not easily obtained). Three types of resources associated with organisations are: *(a)* physical (plant; technology and equipment; geographic location); *(b)* human (employees' experience and knowledge); and *(c)* organisational (structure, systems for planning, monitoring, and controlling activities; social relations within the organisation and between the organisation and external constituencies). HR practices greatly influence an organisation's human and organisational resources and so can be used to gain competitive advantages (Schuler and MacMillan, 1984).

The second theoretical influence is the *behavioural view* based on contingency theory. This view explains practices designed to control and influence attitudes and behaviours, and stresses the instrumentality of such practices in achieving strategic objectives. The *cybernetic system* explains the adoption or abandonment of HR practices resulting from feedback on contributions to strategy. For example, training programmes may be adopted to help pursue a strategy and would be subsequently adopted or abandoned based on feedback. The fourth influence, based on *transaction costs* explains why organisations use control systems such as performance evaluation and reward systems. The argument is that in the absence of performance evaluation systems linked to reward systems, strategies might not be pursued. The other two theories provide explanations for HR practices that are not driven by strategy considerations but based on power and political influences, control of resources *(resource-based theory)* and expectations of social responsibility *(institutional theory)* (Greer, 1995: 107-8).

Implications for HRM Practices

The idea that individual HR practices impacts on performance in an additive fashion (Delery and Doty, 1996) is inconsistent with the emphasis on internal fit in the resource-based view of the firm. With its implicit systems perspective, the resource-based view suggests the importance of "complementary resources", the notion that individual policies or practices "have limited ability to generate competitive advantage" (Barney, 1995:56). This idea, that a system of HR practices may be more than the sum of the parts, appears to be consistent with discussions of synergy, configurations, contingency factors, external and internal fit, holistic approach, etc (Delery and Doty, 1996; Huselid, 1995). Drawing on the theoretical works of Osterman (1987), Sonnenfeld and Peiperl (1988), Kerr and Slocum (1987) and Miles and Snow (1984), Delery and Doty (1996) identified seven practices that are consistently considered strategic HR practices. These are: (1) internal career opportunity; (2) formal training systems (3) appraisal measures; (4) profit sharing; (5) employment security; (6) voice mechanisms; and (7) job definition. There are other SHRM practices that might affect organisational performance. For example, Schuler and Jackson (1987) presented a very comprehensive list of HR practices. However, the seven practices listed by Delery and Doty above appear to have the greatest support across a diverse literature. For example, nearly all of these are also among Pfeffer's (1994) 16 most effective practices for managing people.

An obvious question at this juncture is: How can organisations effectively adopt, implement and maximise HRM practices for valued firm level outcomes? That is, how can firms increase the probability that they will adopt and then effectively implement appropriate HRM practices? Insuring that members of the HRM personnel have the appropriate human capital or competencies has been suggested as one way to increase the likelihood of effective implementation of HRM practices (Huselid, et al., 1997).

Ulrich and Yeung (1989) argue that the future HR professional will need four basic competencies to become partners in the strategic management process. These include business competence, professional and technical knowledge, integration competence and ability to manage change.

On the other hand, the United Kingdom-based Management Charter Initiative (MCI), an independent competence-based management development organisation, identifies seven key roles and required competencies. These include competencies required to manage roles like managing activities, managing resources, managing people, managing information, managing energy, managing quality and managing projects (MCI Mangement Standards, April, 1997). Finally, Huselid, et al., (1997) identified two sets of HR personnel competencies as important for HR personnel: (1) HR professional competencies; and (2) Business-related competencies.

HR professional competence describes the state-of-the-art HR knowledge, expertise and skill relevant for performing excellently within a traditional HR functional department such as recruitment and selection, training, compensation, etc. This competence insures that technical HR knowledge is both present and used within a firm (Huselid, et al., 1997). Business-related *competence* refers to the amount of business experience HR personnel have had outside the functional HR specialty. These capabilities should facilitate the selection and implementation of HRM policies and practices that fit the unique characteristics of a firm including its size, strategy, structure, and culture (Jackson and Schuler, 1995). In other words, these competencies will enable the HR staff to know the company's business and understand its economic and financial capabilities necessary for making logical decisions that support the company's strategic plan based on the most accurate information possible.

Strategic HRM and Organisational Performance

Researchers in SHRM posit that greater use of such practices will always result in better (or worse) organisational performance (Abowd, 1990; Gerhart and Milkovich, 1990; Huselid, 1995; Leonard, 1990; Terpstra and Rozell, 1993). Leonard (1990) found that organisations having long-term incentive plans for their executives had larger increases in return on equity over a four-year period than did other organisations. Abowd (1990) found that the degree to which managerial compensation was based on an organisation's financial performance was significantly related to future financial performance. Gerhart and Milkovich (1990) found that pay mix was related to financial performance. Organisations with pay plans that included a greater amount of performance contingent pay achieved superior financial performance. In combination, these studies indicate that organisations with stronger pay-for-performance norms achieved better long-term financial performance than did organisations with weaker pay-for-performance norms.

Terpstra and Rozell (1993) posited five "best" staffing practices and found that the use of these practices had a moderate and positive relationship with organisational performance. Finally, Huselid (1995) identified a link between organisation-level outcomes and groups of high performance work practices. Instead of focussing on a single practice (e.g., staffing), Huselid assessed the simultaneous use of multiple sophisticated HR practices and concluded that the HR sophistication of an organisation was significantly related to turnover, organisational productivity and financial performance.

In the case of requisite competencies for HR personnel, emerging evidence from empirical research demonstrates the increasing need for HR personnel to have both HR professional and business-related skills and competencies. A survey of HR executives in the US show that HR managers are spending relatively less time in record keeping and auditing, while their time spent in their activities as a business partner have doubled. The survey also revealed that HR managers believe that their HR staffs most important skill needs are team skills, consultation skills and an understanding of business (Noe, et al., 1997).

Managerial competencies particularly in the HR function bring two advantages to the HR function: (1) Enhance the status of the HR department (Barney and Wright, 1988); (2) Act as important influences on the level of integration between HR management and organisation strategy (Golden and Ramanujam, 1985; Ropo, 1993). A study of Singaporean companies found that when HR managers lack the necessary skills to perform their duties competently, line managers and executives take over some of the functions of HR managers (Nee and Khatri, 1999). Research on managerial competencies by Ropo (1993:51) stressed that "the internal dynamism of the HR function serves as the most critical mechanism to keep the integration process going after it has been started under favourable organisational and strategic circumstances". Other studies show that if HR managers can evaluate their priorities and acquire new sets of professional and personal competencies, the HR function would be able to ride the wave of business evolution proudly with other functions in the organisation (Becker and Gerhart, 1996; Ulrich, et al., 1995).

Huselid, et al (1997) conducted an elaborate study on 293 firms in the US to evaluate the impact of human resource managers' professional/technical competencies on HR practices and the latter's impact on organisational performance. Results of the study suggest that consistent with the resource-based view of the firm, there exist a significant relationship between SHRM practices and firm performance. They found that—(1) HR related competencies and, to a lesser extent, business-related competencies increase the extent of effective implementation of SHRM practices; and (2) consistent with recent studies linking HRM activities and firm performance (Arthur, 1994; Cutcher-Gershenfeld, 1991; Huselid, 1995; Huselid and Becker, 1996; MacDuffie, 1995), the study support the argument that investments in human resources are a potential source of competitive advantage. Recent reviews of theoretical and empirical literature (Juhary Ali and Bawa, 1999; Irwin, et al., 1998; Jackson and Schuler, 1995) suggest that a variety of factors affect the relationship between HRM and firm performance. These factors include firm size, technology and union coverage.

The influence of firm size on HRM practices is fully documented in theoretical and empirical studies. For example, institutional theory suggests that larger organisations should adopt more sophisticated and socially responsive HRM practices because they are more visible and are under more pressure to gain legitimacy. Many empirical studies show that firm size is an important variable influencing HRM practices (Ng and Maki, 1993; Wagar, 1998). There are emerging evidences that HR practices may differ in organisations depending on the *level of technological sophistication* in terms of training (Majchrzak, 1988), performance appraisal (Ouchi, 1977, 1980; Snell, 1992) and reward systems (Kaus, 1990; Snell and Dean, 1992). Theoretical and empirical studies also support the position that the presence of specific HRM practices may differ based on the *union coverage* of a firm (Ng and Maki, 1993, Wagar, 1998; Lawler and Mohrman 1987).

CONCLUSIONS

This paper set out as a contribution to the current discourse on the interaction of globalisation and business performance especially with a flavour of the challenges from the perspectives of developing countries such as Malaysia and Nigeria. This paper presents a framework for Strategic Human Resource Management as a response to prepare organisations for the challenges of globalisation. It has been observed that by and large organisations have achieved relatively low levels of effectiveness in implementing Strategic Human Resource Management (SHRM) practices (Huselid, et al., 1997). If the propositions outlined above are supported, then the real challenge for organisations in the era of globalisation is to pay particular emphasis to strengthening their human resources by upgrading the relevant competencies.

As governments and corporate bodies brace up for the new millennium characterised by an ever-increasing global challenge, developing countries have no choice but to develop and continuously upgrade the human resource and business competencies of their workforce. In the case of developing countries, distinct competencies are important to deal with not only the HR issues but also others including partnerships in economic recovery especially in South East Asia, dealing with the "big boys", the fund managers, concerns over possibility of fraud in E-commerce with fast spread of Information Technology and last but not least, implementing prescriptions for recovery and growth taking into consideration the development agenda and unique circumstances of individual countries. Addressing these issues is a necessary step towards facing the challenges of globalisation in to the next millennium.

Human Resource Management (HRM) Practice in India

Despite the tremendous technological advances and rise in production, poverty and hunger, unemployment and underemployment, denial of access to basic amenities to the vast multitudes constitute the fundamental characteristics of the world around. It had been forecast the globalisation would set up a better economic order for harmonious growth and development of the economy, more or less free from tariff barriers, with the free flow of goods and commodities and services, minimising costs and maximising human benefit. Liberalisation of economic system and globalisation of the world economy are essentials of the new economic order. Liberalisation proceeding globalisation proceeds to privatisation. The downsizing of the state, it relies on the production of market forces to promote human development. Whether globalisation has succeeded in realising its lofty objective is the cordial question.

That the Indian economy has not been doing well has been known for long. Reforms initiated to turn it around have not succeeded. A decade is a long enough time for any experiment to bear fruit. What was earlier a slowdown, a fall in the economic growth rate, has now developed into a full-fledged recession. The myth of the new economic policy has been exploded. The so-called strong macroeconomic indicators substantial foreign exchange reserves, bountiful buffer stock of food, even fiscal deficit purportedly being kept within limits, can no longer hide the grim realities, a flambuoyant finance minister had to admit that the current economic slowdown was of grim in nature. The day A.B. Vajpayee was addressing the reconstituted economic advisory council convened to draw up an immediate plan for a salvage operation, the Sensex closed at a near four month low and the Rupee crashed to a new low of Rs. 47.34 with the foreign portfolio investors remitting dollars heavily to their overseal headquarters.

REFORMS: MARGINALISATION OF THE WORKING MASSES IN INDIA

Never before have the Indian working people been so brutally attacked as now; nor has any government been so hostile to its people. The International Labour Organisation (ILO) says that about 5.5 million people have been laid off since the process of liberalisation began in this country. If labour laws are further liberalised, allowing corporates more leeway to restructure, the redundancy figures will get bloated still. Making clear the government's intention of patronising the move for further displacement of labour, the prime minister, addressing the last session of the Indian Labour conference called for the removal of the rigidities in labour laws so that the reform process could pick up momentum. The labour minister made an even more impassioned plea for change in labour laws. Clearly the liberalisation of labour laws, as demanded by corporates—domestic and foreign—is a high priority item on the government's agenda, necessitating the Constitution of a National Commission for Labour in a way that enables the government to issue doctored report. The government bolstered its efforts towards this end by appointing three committees, obviously in expectations that they would provide recommendations on the dotted lines so that the labour law reforms can be carried forward more recklessly. The panel headed by Montok Singh Ahluwalia lost no time in recommending complete freedom to lay-off people. It has further suggested the introduction of short-term employment, with workers hired on contract, liable to be terminated at the completion of the contract without any scope for raising dispute and having no right to claim statutory benefits, While the Geetakrishnan Committee„ proposed a trimming of the government and the reduction its manpower, the task force headed by Rakesh Mohan called for the corporatisation of the Indian railways with a heavy off-loading of the workforce.

Undoubtedly, there is a concerted move to reduce manpower everywhere, irrespective of whether it is in the public or private sector, to cut down labour costs and to pass on the entire burden of the recession on to the shoulders of the working masses. Sweeping changes in labour laws are motivated by the need to ensure easy profits for industry even in a shrinking market. The Government of India, cynically working at the behest of industrial tycoons see to amend Industrial Disputes Act and other labour laws and acting in collusion with corporates to marginalise the working masses.

Jobless growth sinister displacement of labour, random closing down of existing enterprises are the stark and essential features of the present day economic scenario. With mergers and acquisitions too having replaced organic growth, there is further collateral damage in the shape of severe relationalisation of labour. The deceleration in the service sector has led to further job cuts and this is true made the worker's scenario grim.

Some examples will highlight the fearful dimensions of the loss of employment since the current generation of economic reforms was initiated. The minister for heavy industries and public enterprises admitted in Rajya Sabha on February 26, 2001 that, 2,69,708 employees had to leave their jobs in central public sector undertakings till March 21, 2002. Many more have had to opt for VRS subsequently job cuts have been pushed through banks, with around 1,26,000 bank employees leaving their jobs in recent times. Additional and massive job cuts have been planned in government and public sector undertakings. The Indian Railways have publicly announced their decision to off-load 3,00,000 employees in a couple of years. The standing Conference of public Enterprises has estimated that around 30 to 40 per cent of its work force is redundant. In line with these trends, the Central Government has decided to cut its work force by 10 per cent over the next five years. State Government are also following the suit. Madhya Pradesh and Rajasthan have already retrenched thousands of quasi-permanent labour virtually without any compensation.

Private sector job cut plans are equally menacing. The Meltdown in the Information Technology (IT) industry has taken a heavy toll, with no less than 10,000 people losing their jobs recently. A leading IT unit has planned a 35 per cent downsizing. Jobs are set to fall in the cement industry as well. Nearly, 6,000 workers have lost jobs in ACC in the last three years. ACC, Larsen and Tubro and Grasim have planned to off-load 6,000 more. The crisis in the textile industry is well known. Thirty mills have downed shutters this years, pushing the number of closed mills to 383 in March 2001. About 57,000 Jute workers have been badly affected by closure of 16 mills announced by the West Bengal labour minister. The latest economic survey has admitted a sharp decline of employment in the manufacturing sector. In recent times, the Steel Authority of India is all set off-lad 10,000 employees through voluntary retirement scheme. The so called voluntary retirement is nothing but camouflaged retrenchment that is now widely practised with the blessings of the government, the compensation offered being of little benefit under current circumstance of declining returns from the constantly falling interest rates. On top of it all there are nearly 4,00,000 lakh closed enterprises, whose workers have literally been thrown out on the streets.

The recent sample survey by the Confederation of Indian Industry of 989 leading manufacturing units indicate a decline in wave cost from 7.5 per cent of sales in 1991 to 5.6 per cent of saves in 200. Yet another report by the CMIE reveals no corresponding improvement in productivity indicating that the decline in wage cost can only be attributed to a fall in wages, gravely affecting the livelihood of the working masses.

Liberalisation, combined with the recent recession has affected the mental health of a large number of employees in different parts of the country, who are seeking help because of their economic woes in larger numbers, according to a leading psychiatrist in Mumbai, it took Saurav Deshpande two months of a state of joblessness to consider a date with death. Six month earlier, the 28-year old software engineer was on the promising edge of the new millennium, on top of the world. Young and ambitious, with an engineering degree in one pocket and a coveted dotcom job in another, Saurav was ready for marriage. Then came the recession: trips to

Singapore and Russia dried out, work faltered and then petered out. Sleep was the first to desert him; appetite followed and friends melted into the thin air, His engagement was put on hold. Two months later, Saurav found himself on the couch of the psychiatrist, fighting depression, popping anti-depressant pills into his mouth. There are numerous other Saunas. India's commercial capital, with all the its apparent booming private enterprises, its much-vaunted service sector, and the IT industry still aspiring to attain new heights, are all under the dark shadow of recession.

Workers, still not jobless, work under constant threat. Suspension of work, lock-outs and retrenchment are the widely used tools to coerce workers and suppress'and legitimate trade union activities. Unions are not allowed to be formed; leaders are dismissed without even a charge sheet. While police atrocities are on the rise, government Labour departments condone criminality, in fact, collude with the criminals. Violation of labour laws is rampant. Provident fund is misappropriate and dearness allowance frozen. Bonus is not paid and the ESI scheme has all but collapsed. Fringe benefits are curbed, canteens are closed, leave travel concessions are withdrawn and even non-payment of wages by government-owned public sector units are routine. When the government breaks its own laws, the private sector is incited to follow the example with a vengeance. On the other side of this scenario owners become rich.

The number of permanent workers falls, while contract and casual workers rise in numbers. Unnumbered and Unrecorded men and women are inducted for work on paltry payment as delinquency is let loose in a ruthless attack on the working masses. Reform has left them without choice. The demoralised community is compelled to accept underpayment, insecurity and tyranny for bear living. The insensitive economic reforms cannot take a country forward.

The reduction of interest rate on provident fund accumulation, while dealing a crushing blow to the wage earners and salaried middle class of the country, enables management in both the public and the private sector to off-load theirs statutory responsibilities significantly. Coupled with this, there has been the decline of interest rates on small savings and long-term bank deposits, gravely hurting the common man.

Sharp economic changes and dilution labour laws have made women and children more vulnerable to economic insecurity and oppression women, more than men, have lost jobs. Wage discrimination against women has assumed alarming proportions, even discrimination in maternity benefits are being denied and harassment at workplace is on the rise. According to the forum for crèche and children service, a reputed non-government offices and a very small-a minuscule five per cent—in the organised sector can avail of maternity benefit. "The over-whelming majority of working women, nearly 190 millon, work without elementary human rights in the country, thanks to tax laws with employers refusing to comply with the legal provision since these provisions are not backed by financial benefits. The recent phenomenon is that women are extremely afraid of demanding the benefit for fear of losing jobs. Their utter helplessness is graphically portrayed in a report by 'Sanhita' a leading Kolkata, NGO. The report, entitled: "The politics of silence" confirms increasing harassment of working women. It is a direct fall out of job insecurity. The report tells a highly distressing story of Sunita, 24, working in a travelling agency who candidly admitted: "I was pressurised by my boss for a sexual favour. He told me that I would have a great career if I complied with his wishes. The day after my refusal, I was sacked for being incompetent".

According to the report, more than 35 per cent of women acknowledged harassment and a still larger section believes that it existed earlier as well. The survey that commenced in 1998 and was finally complied and published recently, establishes beyond doubt that it is essentially job insecurity that has created the pernicious breeding ground for such harassment.

Once again, stagnating poverty and growing deprivation drive children to work in subhuman conditions. About 65 million children work for eight to 10 hours a day to supplement family incomes because parents cannot earn enough to meet even the bare requirements. The increasing supply, of child labour depresses the general wage level to the great advantage of the exploiter. Essentially, the current model of economic reforms has the recession that it has engendered result in great human distress and led to the economic pauperisation of the working masses. In order to ensure easy profit-making the government has chosen the policy of marginalising the national work force in an act of aggression that the working class has never before experienced in this country.

5

Globalisation and Management of Human Resources in Rural Orissa

Babilata Shroff[♣]

GLOBALISATION AND THE CHANGING BUSINESS ENVIRONMENT

Opening up of the Indian economy to the global market has altered domestic and global market to a great extent. While facing the challenges of globalisation and to attain international competitiveness India needs from its producers higher rates of productiveness, improved quality products and innovations in products and process technology. The weaker organisations of the domestic economy while competing with the efficient MNCs have to restructure and revamp their units with the changing business environment as the MNCs have worldwide popularity and are growing faster due to their worldwide reputation, marketing superiorities, strong financial position, technological superiority and effective product innovations due to their superior research and development. They are also easily penetrating into the Indian market due to our craze for their products.

♣ Smt. Babilata Shroff, Lecturer in Economics, D.A.V. College, Titilagarh, Orissa.

GLOBALISATION AND CHANGING TRENDS IN EDUCATION

Matching with the changes of the post globalisation the higher education system has also changed. Change is occurring faster everyday. Many societies have shifted from "Industrial" era to "Information" era. Total of all human knowledge that was available to an under graduate in 1997 will be less than 1 per cent of that in 2050 (Gandhe, 2002). With the developments in Information and Communication Technologies the learning and training process has changed a lot. Some are:

- ❖ From institution based learning to far learning education with just in time knowledge provisions;
- ❖ From fixed curricula to personalised curricula;
- ❖ From front-ended education to life-long education;
- ❖ From teaching to learning.

These developments are quite effective for learning process by providing the learner freedom to choose what, where and when to learn and from which source. One of the most important features of these emerging technologies is their improved capacity to facilitate learning. Information comes to us with uncanny speeds and ways never before imagined.

With widening of job market after globalisation, tremendous developments in the field of science and technology and emergence of Information Technology, Information Highway, Teletex, Videotex, E-mail, Tele-conferencing(audio-video) and Computer Conferencing, home as well as business users are in a position to get the benefits of idea generation and feedback. Internet leads to an increasingly 'free market' in education, protecting the user from national, state or provincial boundaries.

A PROFILE OF RURAL ORISSA

In this changing business and educational environment, the question arises 'is Orissa in a comfortable position?'. Orissa as a federal state of India achieved a little as compared to some industrially advanced Indian states. In spite of its rich mineral reserves, long coastlines, massive/enormous tourism potential and mass of low cost skilled and unskilled workforce, Orissa is backward even it is at the bottom of the list in terms of per capita income. The magnitude of rural poverty has been the highest all along. The State's economy is too much dependent on agriculture which is again of primitive type. More than 65 per cent of the total working population of the state is engaged in agriculture amd allied activities, which contributes 28 per cent of the State net domestic product. Agriculture which is considered as the mainstay of the economy is still away from modern technology in many parts of the state. On the other hand agriculture, the main employment generator, has also stopped absorbing people though rural population is growing at an alarming rate. The state of Orissa depicts a paradoxical picture of poverty amidst plenty even in this 21st century. There is an urgent need to chalk out and implement a path breaking-metamorphic vision framework to plan, re-structure and re-work the developmental activities/initiatives to help Orissa to realise its optimum growth and project itself as a model state for other states to emulate and prestigiously face the challenges of globalisation.

FLEXIBILITY OF THE RURAL ECONOMY

Even after 60 years of independence and developmental planning, the rural population do not find themselves in the mainstream of development across the country as the basic requirements of life like healthcare, sanitation, quality and level of education, employment and overall quality of life are still in a drastic condition. While we talk of rocketing towards becoming rich, the question arises how far it is possible in the prevailing rural conditions. The march towards a bright future is quicker in urban societies than in rural society.

Since the rural manpower have a dearth of critical skills and knowledge, physical capital—whether indigenous or imported, cannot be productively used; finally it results into breakdown of machines and quick wear out, wastage of materials and components, fall in quality of production and rise in costs. For agricultural workers indiscriminate use of fertilisers, unscientific crop rotation, defective animal rearing, unsystematic land management, etc. In this post globalisation era the tertiary sector has grown rapidly leaving behind the manufacturing sector and far behind the primary sector. The industry/business and education interface is also strengthened. But the agriculture sector has shown no response to these changes. 72 per cent of our brethren live in rural India and a majority of them study in kerosene lanterns and candles. Can we think of the use of computers? Hunger and deprivation are the general issues. Their first struggle is for existence and then comes the question of education and finally higher education. It does not mean that rural India/Orissa lack talent and educated/skilled/efficient manpower. The matter of concern is that the educated, skilled and talented manpower migrate to the urban manufacturing or service sector leaving the remaining rural mass behind. Urban-urban migration i.e. migration of the skilled/educated manpower is considered as a sense of prestige in the society and a case of upward mobility. It is also away from exploitation. Migration of the people in the higher strata of the society is free from headache. On the other hand rural-urban migration of the unskilled labour or manpower from the lower strata of the society is deserting them from their limited assets as well as family. The economic gain is far below the socio-economic exploitation they face. Always there is gain by the elite class- employing units. labour agents, etc. With economic progress and growth of middle class and their aspirations the rural haves migrate to urban centers in search of investment in their children's education or some retail trade as they think it as the best way for their upward mobility. With the growth of private professional educational institutions having an expensive fee structure most of the rural poor aspiring for higher education remain helpless. The rural mass has potentials and intelligence like others, but the pity is: they do not know how to use it effectively. They have resources, knowledge and power, but they need to be motivated to apply the resources effectively. In spite of being the gainers they are the victims of globalisation. Hence there is a need for real knowledge to utilise the resources i.e. efficient management of the resources.

MANAGEMENT OF HUMAN RESOURCES

One of the most important ways of coming out of the clutches of underdevelopment is optimum utilisation of the resources. Among the various types of resources human resources are the most active types as their qualitative and quantitative development are very much required for the proper utilisation of other resources. By human resources we mean the size of population of a country along with its efficiency/ability, educational quality, productivity, organisational ability, skills and technical know-how. There is a need for manpower planning i.e. planning of human resources for meeting the development needs of the economy. Management of human resources simply implies planned development and utilisation of manpower resources i.e. development of top skills for solving the problems faced by the mankind, its habitat and the society. In all the three situations of abundance of resources, scarcity of resources and just required amount of resources HRM has an important role to play.

Management of human resources is required for all classes of business, industry, commerce and polity. Its requirement is more for the rural economy as they are unaware of their potentiality. CEO and HR leaders want to develop people, measure employee engagement, change the performance management system, lunch a culture of coaching, their common purpose, initiate culture change, and so on. All of these are important initiatives that deserve to succeed. On the success of these initiatives depends the image and reputation of the CEO and HR professional. The HR leader must have conceptual clarity in the nature of work, capacity to prioritise in tune with the realities and effective communication. He must have the capacity to checkout initiatives and enhance the engagement of employees in the organisation and thereby prolong their stay with the work.

He must study and benchmark their best practices in employee engagement. The best practices include creating a fun filled work atmosphere, initiative and encouragement to employees providing tea, coffee or juice etc. and some times sharing information, resources and knowledge. Frequent open-houses with employees and discrete one-on-ones could provide clues to gaps in the engagement levels of the engagers themselves. People engagement is the key organisational capability and execution of company objectives.

The most important problem of rural orissa is the existence of old beliefs, ignorance and tolerance. Sustainable development is the slogan of the day which refers to development meeting the needs of the present without comprising the ability of future generation to meet their own needs: we are not even in a position to meet the needs of the present. Fragmented and piece meal efforts will only remain attempts without being translated into outcome and a burden on public exchequer.

In rural Orissa generally we find the existence of skilled as well as unskilled labour and also totally illiterate and so called literate manpower. These area lack manpower posing critical skills and knowledge required, possible alternative production technique market imperfections, opportunities and institutions Human resources are manifested in low level of productivity and limited and unsystematic specialisation. They should be converted into human capital making them skilled in their own trades. The manager whether a Government personnel or non-Government agent must be dedicated in his job and his first duty is to identify the various trades in the rural economy and existing skill. Then either by forming groups or organising them trade wise, sincere efforts could be made to make them aware of their own potentiality and collect informations regarding their indigenous knowledge.

As rural poverty is associated with agricultural growth and the state lack irrigational facility, the farmer face the gambles of monsoon there is every possibility of crop failure. Landlessness, indebtedness and marginal irrigation compel the farmers to migrate or sometimes commit suicide. In this context the rural manpower could be trained to make themselves skilled or upgraded regarding appropriated cropping pattern, use of agricultural technology, mixed cropping techniques, crop rotation, organic farming, crop diversification, scientific weeding, agricultural waste management, upgradation in animal rearing, etc. rather than going for the so-called ABCD—in the educational curricula. They should be taught to integrate the various possible rural activities and use them as a source of their sustainable growth and livelihood security. Education in this sphere will work as "life enhancing" and the human resource manager will play the role of a "force multiplier" accelerating the pace of development. They may be trained and encouraged to go for part/full time engagement in cottage industries or agro processing activities. The most important is education should be taken to their door steps. This may require a group of specially trained teachers, workshops and tools. Higher education for them will be use of computers and then information technology, bio-technology, horticulture, forestry, fishery, weather forecasting etc. The structural difference between the IT sector and Biotechnology sector is existing and the former is always moving faster. Here the integration of these two sectors should be encouraged.

As the rural areas have heterogeneity in various aspects, location specific techniques and curricular should be developed.

A model is prepared for the human resource managers.

1. Policies
2. Cost benefit analysis
3. Linking

4. Identification of area
5. Ordering of processes
6. Best practices

Integration of processes

Effort should be made to shift them from subsistence agriculture to commercialise. In place of low valued products they should go for high valued crops to have income security. Some typical things should be noted for example paddy is the main crop in Orissa. Looking at the conditions required for paddy if absent or deficient they should be encouraged to go for crop diversification. Location specific cropping pattern should be adopted.

As population growth and increasing dependency on land resource are existing in rural areas, effort should be made to absorb the surplus labour inside that area by engaging them either in government works or in self employment programmes. The social scientists should motivate them against suicide. The psychiatrists should motivate them towards healthy living. The manager should encourage research and practical works there. He has to adopt a holistic approach adjusting with the existing infrastructure, human resource, capital and other resources. In a rural atmosphere the manager has to work as catalyst for their speedy upliftment and an instrument for poverty alleviation.

As the rural economy has a rich potentiality, the private domestic investors as well as the TNCs should target it and explore new possibilities.

A separate curricula should be prepared for the women folk and make them come out of the fore walls and realise their internal potentialities. They should be managed to go for studies in health, nutrition, sanitation, stitching, animal rearing, child care, etc. effort should be made on asset formation and capacity building.

Rural tourism potentiality should be exploited and a number of jobs could be created. The rural folk should be given human rights education to make them realise their own rights and raise voice against atrocities and exploitation against them. The cobweb path of development could be checked if the rural mass could know the effects of majority ruled by minority. The manager has to adopt a people centered and people oriented method. While the re-enforcing the national programmes and activities a decentralised method should be adopted.

CONCLUSION

In the context of globalisation the human resource manager has to take decision on local conditions with a global vision. Though the pace of adjustment of the urban/industrialised and developed manpower is easier and quicker, it is not impossible for the rural unorganised mass. A practical and result oriented skill utilisation effort of the manager could work as a precious tool for their survival and growth. It is needed to collectively map the human resource requirements and put forth efforts for streamlining the management system so that skills, knowledge, employability and enterprise evolve for the benefit of the country. We may conclude with Karan Paul, Chairman, Apeejay Surendra Group, "Globalisation has changed the business environment, people live to work harder, longer and there is more pressure to perform", really globalisation demands from the HRM to work in multiple skills, technologies, domain and platforms.

REFERENCES

1. Joseph, Shaji; Power of the People, Political Mobilisation and Guaranteed Employment; *EPW*, Dec. 16, 2006.
2. Kundu, Amitabh and Sarangi, Niranjan: Migration, Employment Status and Poverty: An Analysis Across Urban Centres; *EPW*. January 27, 2007.
3. Gooptu, Nandini; Economic Liberalisation, Work and Democracy: Industrial Decline and Urban Politics in Kolkata; *EPW*, May 26, 2007.
4. Chakrabarti, Anjan and Dasgupta, Bvasdeb: Disinterring the Report of National Commission on Labour: A Marxist Perspective; *EPW*, May 26, 2007.
5. Cohen, Laurie and El-Sawad Amal; Accounting for 'Us'and 'Them': India and UK Customer Service Worker's Reflections on Offshoring; *EPW*, May 26, 2007.
6. Chakrabarti, Manali; Labour and Closure of a Mill: Lives of Workers of a Closed Factory in Kanpur; *EPW*, May 26. 2007.

7. Patra, Digambara; Technological Excellence and Human Resources Development: Twin Mantra of Orissa's Development; *Orissa Vision* 2020.

8. Mukharjee. Kalyan; Asset Management: A Success Story; *The Indian Banker*, Nov. 2006, Vol. 1; No. 11.

9. Mishra, Alok K.; Strategies for Inclusive Growth: Learnıng from Global Experience; *The Indian Banker;* Dec. 2006, Vol. 1, No. 12.

10. Kumar, P. Suresh; Outsourcing in Banking Sector—An Analysis; *The Indian Banker;* April 2006, Vol. 1, No. 4.

11. Investment Climate: India a Low Risk Country for Investment; Page. 54, *Chronicle,* March 2006.

12. Isabelle, Guerin; Augendra, Bhukuth; Parthasarathy; and G. Venkata Subramanian; Labour in Brick Kilns: A Case Study of Chennai; *EPW,* Feb. 17-23, 2007.

13. Mahalingam, S.; Labour Cooperatives in India—A Perspective; *Yojana,* May, 1996.

14. Mallick, Anupriyo; Social Mobilisation: An Empowering Tool for Community Development; *Kurukshetra,* August 2007.

15. Prasad, J. Siva Durga and Sridevi. M. Sandhya; Diversity in Workforce—A Focus on Persons with Disabilities; *Kurukshetra,* August 2007.

16. Satapathy, Sachidananda; Stability and Sustainability of Educated Orissa Unemployed Youth; *Orissa Vision 2020.*

17. Swami Arupananda; Tribal Children and Education in Orissa; *Orissa Vision 2020.* Gandhe, S.K.; Distance Education: New Technologies in the 21st Century.

6

HRM in Higher Education After Globalisation

Challenges and Perspectives

Umesh Chandra Pati♣

There has been phenomenal growth in the higher education sector in the era of globalisation compared with the pre independence era. The objectives of higher education have gradually become more and more precise and as system of governance are developing in the direction of increasing autonomy and accountability. Significant progress has been made in recent years not only in the development and strengthening of higher education in terms of increased student access, strengthened research and post-graduate programmes, more equitable representation of varied social groups, renewed curricula and adoption of new teaching and delivery methods, but in enhanced institutional management and strategic planning capacity as well. The higher education system has been experimenting with management approaches to deal with challenges arising of both internal factors and external factors. The internal factors include changes in

♣ Dr. Umesh Chandra Pati, Senior Lecturer in Economics, Nayagarh Autonomous College, Nayagarh.

academic disciplines and new instructional methods, the external factors include population growth, changing labour market requirements, establishment of open universities and distance learning system as well. Involvement in decision making by all stakeholders has become the need of the hour. To this end a large number of autonomy is being stimulated in the system to encourage freedom to select staff and students, determine the curriculum and degree standards and to allocate funds at the same time being accountable to the system.

Higher education in India is imparted by a plethora of agencies. While the university system falls within the jurisdiction of UGC, different other agencies are there to coordinate the professional institutes. The examples are AICTE for technical and management institution, MCI, ICMR, Indian Nursing Council, PCI, the Bar Council of India, ICAR, ICSSR etc. There are other coordinating agencies like AIU, NAAC etc.

HRM IN HIGHER EDUCATION

HRM can be defined as strategic and coherent approach to the management of organisations' most valuable assets: the people working there who individually and collectively contribute to the achievement of its objective. It encompasses those activities designed to provide for and coordinate the human resources of an organisation.

THE CHALLENGES

The universities epitomise the seat of higher learning in modern education. They have to compete with other non-academic jobs, which are paying high and taking quality workforce from the universities. There is immense competition for scholars and researchers. On one hand there has been depletion in terms of competencies and on the other there are skill shortages in some disciplines. There is limited or no autonomy in implementing proper HR strategy. The crucial HR functions like selection and reward are dependent on regulatory authorities which are outside the domain of universities. Funding not matching the demand for education, large number of classes with high workloads, the bureaucratic hassles, changes in the students' demand etc. need a proper perspective to HRM. HRM will integrate the people, strategy and performance. It will help to build the capacity to conceptualise and support the implementation of significant change.

EMERGING SITUATION

Globalisation has caused multi-directional movements and a forceful revival of the economy. It is now galloping with a growth rate of about 9 per cent. There is every possibility of India emerging as a super power in the next few years. Hence efficient utilisation of existing knowledge base will help to achieve the 11th plan objective of inclusive growth. The knowledge society has two components driven by societal transformation and wealth transformation. The societal transformation is in respect of education, health care, agriculture and good governance. It will lead to more employment generation, high productivity and rural prosperity. Wealth generation will hover around the national competencies in core areas like IT, bio-technology, nano technology, space technology, weather forecasting, disaster management, sustainable development etc. In the new society, knowledge has integrated the economies of the world and made them interdependent and interconnected. Hence there is need for genuine knowledge generated by various institutions with the main objective of inclusive growth and welfare of all.

Since globalisation policies have paved the way to the private sector for more jobs and with the 'no' recruitment policy of the public sector modifications in the curriculum to suit the requirements of the industry has become imperative. After the implementation of the new economic policy, the state is being replaced by the private sector. The entry of private sector to the field of higher education has made it a lucrative commodity to be traded. It has fallen under an international trade category meaning anyone can trade anywhere with education as a thing. Although debatable it is often said that private sectors are more disciplined and efficient than the government sector. This being the case, it is expected that education will be more efficiently and in more disciplined way be managed in the private institutes. Hence a corporate culture will prevail in the private institutes that are absent in the public institutes.

But we have to remember the words told by Adam Smith long back. That it is not from the benevolence of the butcher, the brewer or the baker that we expect our dinner, but from their regard to their own self interest. Here lie all theories of investment by the private sector. Profit or in gentle word return on investment is the ultimate motive. As a consequence of ever increasing marketisation of higher education the basic disciplines like philosophy, history and political science are not offered by the private institutes. This will create an imbalance in higher education for the coming generation. The high tuition fees of higher education in the private sector will only be affordable to the rich. Generating scope for higher education for affordable students at the cost of non-affordable but meritorious students is bound to cast poor figure and accentuate gross inequality. This issue is to be carefully looked into to restore social balance.

Globalisation of Indian economy has compelled organisations to rethink and revitalise their resources to suit the future strategies. It is now widely recognised that transformation is the pre requisite to survival and growth of an organisation. For the human resource function, there could not be a more exciting and challenging opportunity than managing the complexities of change and transformation. The time to respond to globalisation is very little. It is imperative that the organisations evolve a new work culture. Traditional hierarchical organisations must give way to lean and flat organisations with relations based on trust and team work. This will enable to respond to new challenges more swiftly and effectively with commendable accuracy.

THE EFFORTS TO BE UNDERTAKEN

The basic effort is introduction of HRM that is involvement of employees and other constituents in the process. This will ensure excellence in performance and generate efforts for continuous self improvement. People seek increased responsibilities and challenges to attain recognition and growth. The other important factor of HRM is optimum utilisation of existing human resource to improve productivity. The exemplary behaviour and hard work has yielded best results as evident from global players like Ajim Premji, Dr Narayan Murthy, Mr Sunil Bharati Mittal, Dr Pratap Reddy, Mr S Ramadorai and a long list of corporate leaders. All these are possible if we inculcate in them the sense of belongingness to the organisation. As the employees feel alienated in the large organisations, the reversal is possible by making everybody feel important. As has always been experienced, the two ways communication helps the employees to come forward with frank opinions, views, suggestions, criticism and grievances.

A CLEAN ORGANISATION

It is time for the university community in particular and the higher education fraternity in general to wake up to the crisis that has enveloped higher education in India. And this crisis is not just one of shrinking resources, though this is amongst the most critical issues. Fundamentally, it is a crisis of leadership, commitment, vision and imagination. Transparency, character and moral building are the key areas of focus. And these will obviously be brought about by and through the people and fall in the domain of Human Resources. HRM would be in the forefront to conduct training and ensure that employees inculcate and imbibe good values of society and stick to the principles of morality. Simple living and high thinking dictum will hold the key for transformation. In the words of Swami Vivekananda, "India needs to combine western world efficiency with Indian spiritual values". People are honest and worthy of trust. Circumstances may make them otherwise. The growth of institutions of higher learning can be sustained by hard work, farsightedness, good management and above all ethical practices. Men with integrity, inquisitiveness, broad outlook, potentiality, aspirations, awareness and ability are to become the active agents of transformation in the changing scenario.

CONCLUSION

In the changing new world order higher education should equip students not only with generic skills but should tailor them to meet the specific requirement of the society. This is due to the realisation that the economic needs are fast changing and higher education needs to be more useful and usable to prepare the youth to meet the challenges of 21st century. The most important challenge is that of "sustainability" which implies meeting current human needs while preserving the environment and natural resources for the future generations. The challenge is also to reduce disparities through capacity building and providing the poor and the dispossessed access to the knowledge and resources needed for a meaningful life. All these challenges require HRM in the institutions of higher education. Unless it is so done, quality will remain a phantom which may appear here and there without becoming a permanent resident. Quality is not a one shot affair. It is an unending journey. It requires a deliberate and persistent attempt in a systematic way.

7

Comparative Study of Operating Hours, Working Time and Employment

Sai Nrupendra Kumar Dash♣

INTRODUCTION

The present paper examines the literature with a view to determining what links can be found between work patterns (in particular, hours of work and capital operating times) and globalisation. We begin from the premise that, in the present world of global competition, any one country's decision about work patterns and capital operating time cannot be independent of the decisions of other countries. Our expectation, therefore, is that relationships between globalisation, work patterns and/or capital operating hours relationships not only exist, but are likely to be complex, and operate in both directions:

(i) differences in work patterns and capital operating hours impact on the direction and extent of trade and FDl flows (amongst other dimensions of globalisation)

♣ Sai Nrupendra Kumar Dash, PGCMS, SMIT.

(ii) trade and FDI flows (and other dimensions of globalisation) themselves influence the evolution of work patterns across countries over time. While it is an interesting question, the present paper pays little or no attention to the wider debate about the pro's and con's of globalisation *per se*.

Thus, the relationship between the two is likely to be dynamic, with one influencing the other, but also affected by the existence (or absence) of laws and regulations in different countries governing trade/FDI and/or work patterns and operating times. Throughout the remainder of the paper, we maintain the distinction between the direction of causality, even though the perceptions of the way in which the work patterns and capital operating time will evolve and, indeed, be influenced by globalisation, may be an important dimension of the decision to enter a particular market or country.

Article

Globalisation

Globalisation has at least two aspects and, some authors argue, at least three. The first concerns the growth in international trade, which might be referred to more narrowly as "internationalisation", but which nevertheless makes the producers in one country subject to competition from producers in another. The second concerns the growth in multinational producing companies, which we refer to as multinational enterprises (MNEs), in which production *by the same company* takes place in several or many countries, generally in different time zones. The third, and more recent dimension debated in the literature, is the globalisation of technological innovation through the multiplication of R&D centres abroad (Hatzichronoglou, 1999, p. 5) or the sharing of virtual R&D centres by researchers in different countries.

However, we generally understand globalisation to refer to much more than just international trade and multinational companies. To take a more general definition, Guillen (undated), argues that globalisation is both fuelled by and results in the cross-border flows of "goods, services, money, people, information, and culture." The concept of globalisation is often taken as an indication of the effective "shrinking" of the world in both time and spatial dimensions. In addition, globalisation has been associated with a narrowing of the gap in both the framing, interpretation and enforcement of laws.

"Globalisation is neither a monolithic nor an inevitable phenomenon. Its impact varies across countries, societal sectors and time. It is fragmentary, contradictory, discontinuous, even haphazard. Therefore, one needs to be open-minded about its unexpected and unintended consequences, and to the role that agency, interest and resistance play in shaping it."

This diversity of experience is true not only across nation states, but also across sectors, etc. In particular, we lack perspectives that "bridge the micro-macro gap, i.e. move across levels of analysis from the world-system to the nation-state, the industry, sector, community, organisation, and group.

CONCEPTUAL REASONS FOR A RELATIONSHIP BETWEEN WORK PATTERNS AND GLOBALISATION

Work Patterns: A Core Issue

It seems, to the authors at least, that not only are work patterns of different countries a potential determinant of the size, direction and nature of FDI flows (and, thereby, trade flows), but are themselves likely to be modified by the operations foreign-owned subsidiaries. Indeed, it is because the links appear to be crucial that the lack of any direct empirical evidence, as we will shown in the next two sections, seems so surprising. FDI, for example, will normally involve the spatial transfer of a product or process first used (presumably successfully) in the home country. If we accept this premise, then the combination of basic wages, premia payments, overtime and shiftwork, and capital operating times under this initial stage of production are known.

Basic Economics of Optimal Work Patterns: Manufacturing, Utilities and Services

In the simplest case, of say a manufacturing company with zero storage costs (i.e. the product price does not vary over the operating period), but given overtime and shift payments, in the long run, there will be an optimal working period defined by the point at which an additional hour of utilisation of capital has a cost that is just equal to the marginal capital saving of plant (Bosworth and Dawkins, 1981,). The issue is somewhat more complex with multiple varying input prices are introduced into the same model, as the marginal cost of an extra hour of work is formed from a weighted sum of factor inputs which may all be time varying in price (Bosworth and Pugh, 1985a and 1985b). However, the outcome, like the single-varying price model, determines the number of hours of work and the times of day (week or year) at which production take place.

"Many of the empirical disagreements in the literature are primarily due to the various levels of analysis at which different researchers operate."

"There is just the possibility that, while the product or service was not successful in the parent county, it might be seen as being successful if transferred elsewhere."

In practice the whole of the service sector has largely been ignored by the theoretical literature. This may be because it poses a number of problems even more complex than those discussed above, for example:

(i) most service sector outlets will have fixed costs, in the form of physical capital (buildings, vehicles, even certain types of capital—such as computers, etc.). Thus, the concept of marginal capital savings is again appropriate, as it was for the manufacturing and utilities sectors;

(ii) labour costs and other input costs (telephones, electricity, etc.) may also vary with the time of day (week or year) in the service sector.

Relevance of Work Patterns and Capital Operating Times to Globalisation

It is clear that work patterns and capital operating hours will be of central importance to potential foreign investors, perhaps more particularly amongst FDI undertaken for cost reasons than as a means of gaining access to new markets.

In the extreme case, for example, a company operating a continuous process technology requiring a 168 hour operating week, may be prevented from investing in a country which bans night and/or weekend working. In effect, any form of restriction that prevents continuous working is equivalent to saying that the marginal cost of an extra hour becomes infinite and, by definition, further expansion of the hours of working (to more "unsocial times") will be halted at that point. In the general case, a company wishing to invest abroad will need to recalculate the costs of production in the light of the system of work patterns and operating times (including various restrictions and premia payments) in the potential host country. The only instance that such a recalculation would not be required would be if:

(i) in the case of manufacturing companies, all of the labour market conditions were identical across countries (in the case of zero storage costs). In other words, normal hours, basic wage rates, overtime premia, shift premia, fixed capital costs, etc. would all need to be identical;

(ii) in the case of utilities and services, which are subject to peak-load issues, this would also require that the pattern of demand over the day (week or year) were also identical.

INFLUENCES ON GLOBALISATION

Broad Range of Influences

In this section we deal with the various influences that have driven the globalisation process. In doing so, we have been selective, not only because the globalisation process means different things to different people (often for entirely legitimate reasons), but also because our principal focus is on the role that might be played by work patterns and capital operating times in directing the flows. On the other hand, we cannot focus on work patterns and capital operating times alone—these neither operate in a vacuum nor can they be considered as exogenous to the process.

Pervasive Global Role of Technological Change

"The extent to which international trade is a controlled transaction within individual firms is tellingly large. The evolution of global economic systems increasingly blurs the importance of national borders, motivates the reallocation of productive resources worldwide and fosters ever more tightly woven fabrics of global interdependence."

As continued transnational integration continues, it becomes less and less appropriate to view production activities and the associated jobs simply as geographically static pyramids of companies engaged in assembling components and parts and delivering services. Within global production regimes, research, development, and design activities are continuously redistributed within and among firms in many different countries to take advantage of technical specialties of the different internal components or external participants. Industrial activities become grand endeavours cutting across national boundaries. They seek competitive advantages by utilising the lowest-cost and highest-quality production, regardless of geographic location. Firms that do not won't survive in the global marketplace.

Influences on the Foreign Investment Decision

The issue of the factors that appear to be important in determining the company's decision to undertake foreign investment. Again, some care has to be taken in the interpretation of these findings, as they appear to particularly focus on FDI, rather than the other modes of entry and broader forms in which a firm becomes involved in "globalising" its activities. In addition, we make a further distinction between the comparative competitive advantages of the firm itself, *vis a vis* the advantages that the particular host country has to offer.

Competitive Advantages of the Potential Parent

The results indicate that the relative advantages of the parent company appear to differ depending upon product area (Purcell, et al. 1998, p. 4). In addition, of course, the precise advantages or their relative importance would almost certainly be different for companies choosing a different method of entry into Australia (i.e. via franchising, licensing, etc.) and are likely to differ for companies from other countries.

Features of the Host Country Influencing Foreign Investment

In this section, we attempt to provide a broad summary of the factors that a potential foreign investor would take into account in considering entry into a particular country. This discussion is based around a report on the determinants of FDI flows, by the UK Overseas Development Institute (1997):

(i) ***Size of the market:*** Econometric studies have generally found a significant correlation between FDI and the size of the market, usually measured by GDP or average income levels and their growth rates;

(ii) ***Openness and trade blocs:*** Survey results indicate that FDI is also more extensive in "open" (i.e. trade oriented) economies (Singh and Jun, 1995), with export activity encouraging FDI inflows;

(iii) ***Labour costs and productivity:*** While we will return to the issue of labour costs, productivity and other aspects of the labour market, it is interesting to note that that empirical research reports relative labour costs to be important in determining FDI, and more particularly so in labour-intensive and export-oriented sectors. The decision to invest in a number

of countries, such as China and Vietnam, has been driven in part by the relatively low wage rate—whereas the greater labour market rigidities and higher wages (at least in the formal sector) appear to have been a deterrent to investment in India (especially in export sectors). While wages are important, they should be judged against the backdrop of labour quality—other things being equal (i.e. wage rates), the skills of the labour force are expected to have an impact on the location of FDI. In particular, the lack of particular skills, such as engineers and technical (as well as managerial skills) are reported to hold back potential foreign investment, especially in manufacturing;

(iv) Political risk: There are various measures of risk, of which political is clearly an important component, particularly amongst the less developed countries; higher risk is linked to a lower propensity to invest. In some instances, however, the possession of abundant natural resources has been more than enough to off-set even high levels of political instability (as has been witnessed historically in Nigeria and Angola). In addition, to some extent, companies can take their own measures (i.e. in infrastructure and security) to reduce the risk;

(v) Infrastructure: In the present study, we extend the discussion of the original ODI paper, to make a clearer distinction between the tangible and intangible (*physical* and *virtual*) infrastructures as perceived by potential foreign investors:

(a) Physical Infrastructure: The early location of FDI in China was linked to the existence of transport facilities and availability of suitable ports. While, the lack of infrastructure is cited as one of the major constraints amongst low-income countries, it can also offer potential for attracting FDI where the host government enables a greater participation of the

foreign partner(s) in the development and running of the infrastructure sector. The impact of the public infrastructure on the performance of firms and the economy in general has been the subject of considerable economic investigation;

(b) *Virtual Infrastructure:* While, by infrastructure, we normally immediately think of roads, railways, etc., the concept is much broader and also relates to the virtual or intangible systems that exist within a country (or internationally). There are many aspects of the "intangible" infrastructure, in particular.

(vi) ***Incentives and operating conditions:*** While the ODI do not state this explicitly, most FDI appears to be tied-up with some form of government incentive. Such incentives may need to be greater the greater the comparative disadvantages of the location concerned, although the country's ability to offer such incentives may be inversely related to the degree of comparative disadvantage. According to ODI, however, "Most...empirical evidence supports the notion that specific incentives such as lower taxes have no major impact on FDI, particularly when they are seen as compensation for continuing comparative disadvantages." It is clear, however, that improvements leading to "good business practices" have a positive effect, such as the changes in China following the "open-door" policy. Other incentives in China, India and other countries have included the relaxation of the regulations on foreign investment;

(vii) ***Privatisation:*** While privatisation has been a positive influence on foreign investment, it's impact has been lessened because it is a "highly political issue" and, thus, tied to the broader question of political instability (i.e. in this instance, major changes in government policy, which may still be a result of the democratic process, such as a switch from a right-to left-wing government). Privatisation has also been associated with labour unrest in most countries, not least in the case of India, where privatisation has been viewed as threatening existing jobs and employment rights.

(viii) ***Financial Markets and Funding of Private Sector Activities:*** The poorly-developed financial sector both limits policies of privatisation and acts more generally to discourage foreign investors. However, it should be borne in mind that this argument is undermined by the fact that the larger MNEs will often have access to the cheapest global sources of finance.

Labour, Work Patterns and Capital Operating Times

Many less developed and developing countries, however, still suffer from a lack of transparency in investment approval procedures, as well as excessive bureaucracy, which is also open to issues of bribery and corruption. The ODI (1997) paper gives examples of the impact of bureaucratic problems.

Efficiency Labour and Unit Labour Costs

We have already discussed on the significant role of productivity and labour costs. The nature and rate of technological advance often means that, where natural resources are not a major issue, production can be replicated virtually anywhere (White and White, 1997). Thus, large MNEs can relocate in response to favourable changes in a variety of factors, including, exchange rates, government policies, labour and product markets. Given the relative immobility of' labour, globalisation of' production places educated and trained workers in one country in direct competition with similar workers elsewhere in the world. Thus, the natural flow of production, other things equal, is towards countries with: (i) lower labour costs (and standards of living), given the "quality" of the potential workforce; (ii) higher quality of labour, given the costs of labour.

Labour Market Flexibility

Labour market flexibility is a complex, multi-dimensional concept, which include a wide range of elements: (i) wage rates (i.e. wage flexibility, such as performance related pay); (ii) other labour costs (i.e. hiring and firing regulations and associated costs); (iii) working time (i.e. cultural, legal, etc. provisions relating to the ability to vary the length of working day, the times at which people can work) and the associated premia payments (i.e. the existence of set rules with respect to overtime, shift or other unsocial hours premia); (iv) retirement age (i.e. ability to retire early, employer pension contributions, etc.); (v) skill versatility (i.e. the existence of different skills and the ability and willingness to undertake multi-tasking); (vi) etc.

Role of Work Patterns and Capital Operating Times

Perhaps the first thing to establish is that the FDI and related globalisation literatures appear to say relatively little about the work patterns and capital operating times (i.e. the rules, regulations, premia, etc.) that they would like to see in the potential host country. The earlier discussion suggested that the empirical literature had focused on the role of unit labour costs, which is a reflection of real wages (including "on-costs", such as employment taxes paid by employers) and labour productivity. These two factors say little about work patterns, *per se*. The degree to which a given product can be produced economically depends upon underlying temporal variations in the demand for the product or service, and the associated variations in supply factors. Thus, the degree to which a given product or service can be introduced into another country will not only depend on the overall averages of wages and labour productivity, but: (i) the rules and regulations regarding hours of work, operating times, etc.; (ii) temporal shifts in the supply of labour or other factors that give rise either to premia or time-of-use tariffs, or difficulties in recruitment or access to key resources at certain times of the day, week or year); (iii) the importance of the temporal distribution of production for total factor productivity, total unit costs and overall revenues.

IMPACT OF GLOBALISATION

Introduction

It is also very important to discuss the impact of globalisation on work patterns, capital operating times and on broader labour market rewards to the globalisation process. Again, the impacts of globalisation are much broader than the remit of the present paper, for example, relating to broader social welfare issues. In addition, the growing role of foreign trade and investment is linked to more recent developments in the literature, where globalisation is associated with inter-firm alliances and information flows.

Globalisation and Management

One response to this is to use expatriate managers to control the operations of the foreign subsidiary. The adoption of expatriate managers may also be an indication that the company is attempting to facilitate the transfer of operating procedures and/or work patterns from the parent to the foreign subsidiary.

Globalisation, HRM and Management Practices

There are extensive discussions of the transfer of HRM practices from parents to subsidiaries, although, as will become apparent below, these only touch on the issue of the transfer of working practices and capital operating times. According to Purcell, *et al.* (1998, p.3), exploitation of the competitive advantages of parent requires the transfer of both management and HRM practices to the affiliate, but not necessarily all of them.

While their survey of 69 Japanese subsidiaries in Australia confirms the division of what is transferred and what is not (i.e. the incentive structures are not replicated in the Australian subsidiaries), nevertheless, there was some attempt by the Japanese company to move in this direction (*op cit.* p. 14). In particular, the researchers found a strong corporate commitment to provide high levels of job security, although not "life-long" employment.

One possible way in which to explore the extent to which foreign owned or controlled enterprises are integrating with the local market is to examine whether they are taking up local initiatives. In the UK, for example, it is possible to examine if foreign affiliates have been participating in a UK initiative to improve training and standards of staff quality—the so-called Investors in People Initiative. It can be seen from the first column of results that, while nearly 24 per cent of UK owned or controlled enterprises in England were accredited, the same was only the case for 14 per cent of wholly foreign owned or controlled enterprises (with joint-enterprises falling between the two). The same result applies to those currently implementing IiP, although the percentages are much lower. However, a higher proportion of jointly-owned or controlled enterprises are currently considering adoption. It would be interesting to extend these results to the adoption of ISO 9000 and 14000.

Globalisation and Technological Change

We argued strongly that technological change was an important influence on the extent of globalisation, both from an individual firm perspective (i.e. in the context of it's comparative advantage over other companies through it's superior product or process technology) or from an overall perspective (i.e. as the nature of technologies that have become available, such as ICTs, have increased the efficiency of global operations). Thus, we would expect that certain MNEs will be involved in a variety of technology transfer activities that will benefit the host country both directly and via spillover effects.

Compensation Packages

Remuneration

Compensation packages for the foreign employees has been the subject of extensive research over many years (see, for example, Dunning, 1981, pp. 272-303—this study also provides a brief review of the earlier literature, *op cit.* p. 274). Here we make a distinction again between wages and broader remuneration of employees and the work patterns that would form part of their broader conditions of employment/compensation package. Given the relative ease of access to wage data, most of the research in this area has focussed on this narrower aspect of the overall package. Nevertheless, even this area of comparison is fraught with difficulties. For example, even if it is possible to control for the occupation and nature of the job, there are issues in valuing non-monetary benefits, and converting all values to a common unit of measurement such as purchasing power parities.

It is clear that we would anticipate lower wages in the host than the parent country, at least where lower labour costs were an important motivation for the foreign investment—although this may not be the case where there are other grounds for the investment. There is also the issue of the relative wages of the employees of the foreign owned enterprise and other workers in the host country.

Employment Stability

One of the key debates about the conditions of employment amongst MNE affiliates has concerned the stability of employment—the worry is that, if the MNE moves into a country because of particular, beneficial conditions at a given point in time, it may equally move out as the prevailing conditions turn adverse. Of course, this fails to recognise the sunk costs of MNEs in establishing affiliates or the range of conditions over which such an affiliate would continue to make a positive contribution to the overall Group. Dunning reviews what he describes as the "patchy" empirical evidence. Thus there is no consensus in the empirical results, in part because many relate to particular sectors or host countries (which have been differentially hit by the economic cycle). We have already noted, that, whilst Japanese parents did not attempt to introduce "life-time" employment policies amongst their Japanese affiliates, there was evidence that they attempted to lay emphasis on job security.

In addition to the diversity of influences, as Dunning points out, the degree of stability is not exogenously given, but driven by the efforts of particular government or regional bodies (such as the Scottish Development Council) to both attract inward investment (new and extensions to existing) and to prevent the destruction or outward movement of jobs. Again, the issue has both a private and social impact, with the latter accentuated by the multiplier and accelerator effects of such investment and employment.

Training Practices

Dunning argues that there is a substantial body of information about the training activities of MNEs. From the MNE's perspective, the extent to which it wishes to invest in training will depend a wide variety of factors, "...its philosophy and general strategy towards its foreign operations; the nature of its long-term resource commitments and the length of its involvement in that country; the nature of the activities in which it is engaged, and particularly the demands they make of human resources; the availability and quality of local training institutions; the attitude and competence of the investing firms to in-house training; its market (or expected market) share; and the role played by government in promoting in-house and other kinds of training programmes."

GLOBALISATION, WORK PATTERNS AND CAPITAL OPERATING TIMES

Knowledge-based and Traditional Production and Services

In this section, we attempt to separate out the discussion of the more traditional production activities (i.e. involving the production of tangible outputs), with at least the extreme case of the production of intangible outputs—that associated with the production of knowledge. In particular, we explore the knowledge production area using the example of formal

R&D, although it is likely to be relevant to a wide variety of areas where intangible outputs are produced.

Knowledge-based Production and Formal R&D

One of the benefits of globalisation in its broadest sense is the *potential* access to knowledge and advanced technologies given to less developed countries by various forms of technology transfer.

One of the crucial issues from a developing country perspective is the location of "high-level activities". While the product life cycle of traditional manufactured goods may give rise to lower-skill level employment opportunities that exploit the comparatively low labour costs of developing countries, it is also important that (as the host country develops) the level of technology transfer and the level of knowledge or skill required increases, allowing wage levels to rise commensurately. Some of the highest-level activities, such as R&D, which are almost entirely knowledge-based (i.e. involve little if any tangible production activities) are, in principle, released from any spatial constraints, for example, of the location of fixed plant and machinery, raw materials or even (to some extent) markets. Much of the debate has surrounded the extent to which such activities have been concentrated solely in the parent country, and the extent to which it has moved out to other countries in which the enterprise operates.

CONCLUSION

Importance of Globalisation for Work Patterns

Far from being a topic of narrow and minor concern, the impact of globalisation on work patterns and capital operating hours is an extensively debated topic. The potential impact of globalisation on the work patterns of particular groups in society is well-recognised, particularly from the point of the poorer economies. These issues are also tied up with the debate about the implications of globalisation for the distribution of income. At first sight, one of the benefits of globalisation appears to be greater equality, as demand is transferred from the higher to the lower income countries. However, the evidence to date suggests that this might not be the case either within countries or across countries and, as a reMore contentiously, Weisbrot, *et al.* (2000) argue that the disenchantment arises not only with the failure of the IMF and World Bank to distribute the returns from growth, but to actually deliver growth at all, with the vast majority of countries' performance being worse in the last two decades than the two previous decades. sult, the International Monetary Fund and the World Bank, have come under increasing criticism in recent years.

More contentiously, Weisbrot, et al. argue that the disenchantment arises not only with the failure of the IMF and World Bank to distribute the returns from growth, but to actually deliver growth at all, with the vast majority of countries' performance being worse in the last two decades than the two previous decades. They do not, however, see the observed patterns imposed as a necessary consequence of globalisation, other patterns could have been adopted given the political will. While the power of the less developed world has been insufficient to mould the outcome, the same might be said of parts of the developed world. The literature is, for example, concerned with the extent to which existing national regulatory and union structures have been able to cope with and adapt to the globalisation process. The answer appears to be that, like governments themselves, unions have found it difficult to meet the new challenges posed by globalisation (especially at times, as in the case of the UK, when the unions were themselves under pressure of restrictions by national governments).

REFERENCES

Albrow, M. (1997). *The Global Age.* Stanford (California): Stanford UP.

Aoki, M. (1988). *Information, Incentives and Bargaining in the Japanese Economy.* Cambridge: Cambridge UP.

Aoki, M. (1990). "Towards an Economic Model of the Japanese Firm". *Journal of Economic Literature.* Vol. XXVIII. March. pp. 1-27.

Berndt, E.R. and B. Hansson (1992). "Measuring the Contribution of Public Infrastructure Capital in Sweden". *Scandinavian Journal of Economics.* Vol. 94. Supplement. pp. S151-S 168.

Bhattacharya, A. Montiel, P.J. and Sharma, S. (1996) *Private Capital Flows to Sub-Saharan Africa: An Overview of Trends and Determinants,* Unpublished Paper, World Bank, Washington DC

Boghani, A.B., A.I. Onassis, A. Benabadji, C.L.A. Bijl and S. Bone (2000). *Prism.* Arthur Little. First Quarter. pp. 35-49.

Bosworth, D.L. and C.A. Pugh (1985a). "Industrial and Commercial Demand for Electricity by Time of Day". *Energy Journal.* Vol. 65. No. 3. pp. 101-7.

Bosworth, D.L. and C.A. Pugh (1985b). "Optimal Capital Utilisation and Shiftworking". *Scandinavian Journal of Economics.* Vol. 87. No. 4. pp. 658-667.

Bosworth, D.L. and D. Yang (2000). *International Business Review.*

Broadman, H.G. and Sun, X. (1997) *The Distribution of Foreign Direct Investment in China,* Policy Research Working Paper No. 1720, World Bank, Washington DC.

Burton, Bendiner (1987). *International Labour Affairs:* The World Trade Unions and the *MNEs.* Oxford: Clarendon Press.

Castells, M. (1996). *The Rise of the Network Society.* Cambridge (Mass.): Blackwell.

Davies, R. (1999). Employer Provided Training within the European Union: A Comparative Review. Working Paper No. 17-99. LEO-CRESEP. Faculé de Droit, d'Economie et de Gestion d'Oleans. Orléans.

Dawkins, P. and M. Simpson (1994). "Work, Leisure and the Competitiveness of Australian Industry". *International Journal of Management.* Vol. 15. Nos. 9-10. pp. 38-76.

Dedoussis, V. (1994). "The Core Workforce-Peripheral Workforce Dichotomy and the Transfer of Japanese Management Practices". In N. Campbell and F. Burton (eds.) *Japanese Multinationals. Strategies in Management in the Global Kaisha.* London: Routledge. pp. 186-217.

Dunning, J.H. (1981). *International Production and the Multinational Enterprise.* London: George Allen and Unwin. (Chapter 10,

"Employee Compensation in US Multinationals and Indigenous Firms: and Exploratory Micro/Macro Analysis", pp. 272-303)

Galbraith, J.K. (1998). "Globalisation and Pay". Remarks to the American Philosophical Society. November.

Griliches, Z. (1992). "The Search for R&D Spillovers". *Scandinavian Journal of Economics.* Vol. 94. Supplement. pp. S29-S48.

Griliches, Z. (1995). "R&D and Productivity: Econometric Issues and Measurement Issues". In P. Stoneman (ed.) *Handbook of the Economics of Innovation and Technological Change.* Oxford: Blackwell. pp. 52-89.

8

The Role of Human Resources After Globalisation

T. Srinibas Dora[♣]
Rabi Narayan Misra[♠]

INTRODUCTION

The current financial crisis, which has engulfed Asia since July 1997 and has subsequently spread to Russia and Brazil, is one of the most pressing challenges facing countries and businesses in today's global business environment. Most of the response to the financial crisis has focussed on macroeconomic aspects and there is relatively little research on the role of human resources. Secondly, the issue of globalisation has been addressed predominantly in, and with respect to, the developed economies of World. This paper is an attempt to address these two limitations since the human factor is one of the key issues in the new era of globalisation (Hassan, 1992; Sims and Sims, 1995). The primary objective of this paper therefore is to present a conceptual framework

♣ Mr. T. Srinibas Dora is a Research Scholar,
E-mail: srinibasdora_1985@yahoomail.co.in

♠ Dr. R.N. Misra, Professor—MBA, SMIT- BPUT- Ankushpur, Berhampur.

for strategic management of human resources as a response to the growing interaction of globalisation and business performance.

Three central arguments made in this paper are:

1. That a great deal of evidence has accrued to suggest that changes taking place in the global business environment often are not accompanied by complementary changes in human resource management practices leading to a situation whereby the failure of some firms is due to the mismanagement of people rather than to problems with technical systems;
2. That this is because organisations have achieved relatively low levels of effectiveness in implementing Strategic Human Resource Management (SHRM) practices. This is particularly the case in emerging economies of developing countries like India, Nigeria, Malaysia, and other countries that are exposed to the challenges and opportunities of globalisation;
3. That in order to manage employees for competitive edge in a period of globalisation, human resource personnel must possess competencies relevant for effective implementation of such strategic HRM policies and practices.

HRM ISSUES AND CHALLENGES IN GLOBAL MARKETS

The coming of the 21st century globalisation poses distinctive HRM challenges to businesses especially those operating across national boundaries as multinational or global enterprises. Global business is characterised by the free flow of human and financial resources especially in the developed economies. Developments are opened to uplift new markets. It needs to manage human resources effectively to gain competitive advantage in the global market place. To achieve this, organisations require an understanding of the factors that can determine the effectiveness of various HR practices and approaches. This is because countries differ along a number of dimensions that influence the attractiveness of Direct Foreign Investments in each country. These differences determine the economic viability of building an operation in a foreign country and they have a particularly strong impact on HRM in that operation. A number of factors that affect HRM in global markets are identified: (1) Culture; (2) Economic System; (3) Political System—the legal framework; and (4) Human capital. Consistent with the scope of the present paper, only one dimension is treated—human capital (the skills, capabilities or competencies of the workforce). This is in consonance with the believe that competency-based human resource plans provide a source for gaining competitive advantage and for countries profoundly affect a foreign country's desire to locate or enter that country's market.

In the case of developing countries, globalisation poses distinct challenges to governments, the private sector and organised labour. These challenges, which must be addressed through a strategic approach to human resource management, include: (1) Partnership in economic recovery especially in South East Asia; (2) Dealing with the "big boys", the fund managers; (3) Concerns over possibility of fraud in E-commerce (such as issues of confidence and trust); and (4) Implementing prescriptions for recovery and growth taking into consideration the development agenda and unique circumstances of individual country.

STRATEGIC HRM AS A RESPONSE TO THE CHALLENGES OF GLOBALISATION

Strategic Human Resource Management (SHRM) involve a set of internally consistent policies and practices designed and implemented to ensure that a firm's human capital (employees) contribute to the achievement of its business objectives.

SHRM refers to "the pattern of planned human resource deployments and activities intended to enable an organisation to achieve its goals". To sum up, it appears that some of the frequently cited fundamental elements of SHRM in the literature are: SHRM practices are macro-oriented, proactive and long term focussed in nature; views human resources as assets or investments not expenses; implementation of SHRM practices bears linkage to organisational performance; and focussing on the alignment of human resources with firm strategy as a means of gaining competitive advantage (Nee and Khatri, 1999:311).

A. Theoretical Foundations of Strategic HRM

Several theoretical perspectives have been developed to organise knowledge of how HR practices are impacted by strategic considerations as briefly described below. Wright and McMahan (1992) have developed a comprehensive theoretical framework consisting of six theoretical influences. Four of these influences provide explanations for practices resulting from strategy considerations. These include, among others, the resource-based view of the firm and behavioural view. The two other theories provide explanations for HR practices that are not driven by strategy considerations: (1) Resource Dependence; and (1) Institutional Theory.

The *resource-based theory of the firm* blends concepts from organisational economics and strategic management (Barney, 1991). This theory holds that a firm's resources are key determinants of its competitive advantage. Firms can develop this competitive advantage only by creating value in a way that is difficult for competitors to imitate. Traditional sources of competitive advantage such as financial and natural resources, technology and economies of scale can be used to create value. However, the resource-based argument is that these sources are increasingly accessible and easy to imitate. Thus they are less significant for competitive advantage especially in comparison to a complex social structure such as an employment system. If that is so, human resource policies and practices may be an especially important source of sustained competitive advantage (Jackson and Schuler, 1995; Pfeffer, 1994). Specifically, four empirical indicators of the potential of firm resources to generate competitive advantage are: value, rareness, limitability and substitutability (Barney (1991). In other words, to gain competitive advantage, the resources available to competing firms must be variable among competitors and these resources must be rare (not easily obtained). Three types of resources associated with organisations are: (a) physical (plant, technology and equipment; geographic location); (b) human (employees' experience and knowledge); and (c) organisational (structure, systems for planning, monitoring, and controlling activities, social relations within the organisation and between the organisation and external constituencies). HR practices greatly influence an organisation's human and organisational resources and so can be used to gain competitive advantages (Schuler and MacMillan, 1984).

The second theoretical influence is the *behavioural view* based on contingency theory. This view explains practices designed to control and influence attitudes and behaviours, and stresses the instrumentality of such practices in achieving strategic objectives. The *cybernetic system* explains the adoption or abandonment of HR practices resulting from feedback on contributions to strategy. For example, training programmes may be adopted to help pursue a strategy and would be subsequently adopted or abandoned based on feedback. The fourth influence, based on *transaction costs* explains why organisations use control systems such as performance evaluation and reward systems. The argument is that in the absence of performance evaluation systems linked to reward systems, strategies might not be pursued. The other two theories provide explanations for HR practices that are not driven by strategy considerations but based on power and political influences, control of resources *(resource-based theory)* and expectations of social responsibility *(institutional theory)* (Greer, 1995: 107-8).

B. Implications for HRM Practices

The idea that individual HR practices impacts on performance in an additive fashion (Delery and Doty, 1996) is inconsistent with the emphasis on internal fit in the resource-based view of the firm. With its implicit systems perspective, the resource-based view suggests the importance of "complementary resources", the notion that individual policies or practices "have limited ability to generate competitive advantage" (Barney, 1995:56). This idea, that a system of HR practices may be more than the sum of the parts, appears to be consistent with discussions of synergy, configurations, contingency factors, external and internal fit, holistic approach, etc (Delery and Doty, 1996; Huselid, 1995). Drawing on the theoretical works of Osterman (1987), Sonnenfeld and Peiperl (1988), Kerr and Slocum (1987) and Miles and Snow (1984), Delery and Doty (1996) identified seven practices that are consistently considered strategic HR practices. These are: (1) internal career opportunity; (2) formal training systems; (3) appraisal measures; (4) profit sharing; (5) employment security; (6) voice mechanisms; and (7) job definition. There are other SHRM practices that might affect organisational performance. For example, Schuler and Jackson (1987) presented a very comprehensive list of HR practices. However, the seven practices listed by Delery and Doty above appear to have the greatest support across a diverse literature. For example, nearly all of these are also among Pfeffer's (1994) 16 most effective practices for managing people.

An obvious question at this juncture is: How can organisations effectively adopt, implement and maximise HRM practices for valued firm level outcomes? That is, how can firms increase the probability that they will adopt and then effectively implement appropriate HRM practices? Insuring that members of the HRM personnel have the appropriate human capital or competencies has been suggested as one way to increase the likelihood of effective implementation of HRM practices (Huselid, *et al.*, 1997).

Ulrich and Yeung (1989) argue that the future HR professional will need four basic competencies to become partners in the strategic management process. These include business competence, professional and technical knowledge, integration competence and ability to manage change.

On the other hand, the United Kingdom-based Management Charter Initiative (MCI), an independent competence-based management development organisation, identifies seven key roles and required competencies. These include competencies required to manage roles like managing activities, managing resources, managing people, managing information, managing energy, managing quality and managing projects (MCI Mangement Standards, April, 1997). Finally, Huselid, *et al.*, (1997) identified two sets of HR personnel competencies as important for HR personnel: (1) HR competencies; and (2) Business-related competencies.

HR professional competence describes the state-of-the-art HR knowledge, expertise and skill relevant for performing excellently within a traditional HR functional department such as recruitment and selection, training, compensation, etc. This competence insures that technical HR knowledge is both present and used within a firm (Huselid, *et al.*, 1997). *Business-related competence* refers to the amount of business experience HR personnel have had outside the functional HR specialty. These capabilities should facilitate the selection and implementation of HRM policies and practices that fit the unique characteristics of a firm including its size, strategy, structure, and culture (Jackson and Schuler, 1995). In other words, these competencies will enable the HR staff to know the company's business and understand its economic and financial capabilities necessary for making logical decisions that support the company's strategic plan based on the most accurate information possible.

C. Strategic HRM and Organisational Performance

Researchers in SHRM posit that greater use of such practices will always result in better (or worse) organisational performance (Abowd, 1990; Gerhart and Milkovich, 1990; Huselid, 1995; Leonard, 1990; Terpstra and Rozell, 1993).

Leonard (1990) found that organisations having long-term incentive plans for their executives had larger increases in return on equity over a four-year period than did other organisations. Abowd (1990) found that the degree to which managerial compensation was based on an organisation's financial performance was significantly related to future financial performance. Gerhart and Milkovich (1990) found that pay mix was related to financial performance. Organisations with pay plans that included a greater amount of performance contingent pay achieved superior financial performance. In combination, these studies indicate that organisations with stronger pay-for-performance norms achieved better long-term financial performance than did organisations with weaker pay-for-performance norms.

Terpstra and Rozell (1993) posited five "best" staffing practices and found that the use of these practices had a moderate and positive relationship with organisational performance. Finally, Huselid (1995) identified a link between organisation-level outcomes and groups of high performance work practices.

Instead of focussing on a single practice (e.g., staffing), Huselid assessed the simultaneous use of multiple sophisticated HR practices and concluded that the HR sophistication of an organisation was significantly related to turnover, organisational productivity and financial performance.

In the case of requisite competencies for HR personnel, emerging evidence from empirical research demonstrates the increasing need for HR personnel to have both HR professional and business-related skills and competencies. A survey of HR executives in the US show that HR managers are spending relatively less time in record keeping and auditing, while their time spent in their activities as a business partner have doubled. The survey also revealed that HR managers believe that their HR staffs most important skill needs are team skills, consultation skills and an understanding of business (Noe, *et al.*, 1997).

Managerial competencies particularly in the HR function bring two advantages to the HR function: (1) Enhance the status of the HR department (Barney and Wright, 1988); (2) Act as important influences on the level of integration between HR management and organisation strategy (Golden and Ramanujam, 1985; Ropo, 1993). A study of Singaporean companies found that when HR managers lack the necessary skills to perform their duties competently, line managers and executives take over some of the functions of HR managers (Nee and Khatri, 1999). Research on managerial competencies by Ropo (1993:51) stressed that "the internal dynamism of the HR function serves as the most critical mechanism to keep the integration process going after it has been started under favourable organisational and strategic circumstances". Other studies show that if HR managers can evaluate their priorities and acquire new sets of professional and personal competencies, the HR function would be able to ride the wave of business evolution proudly with other functions in the organisation (Becker and Gerhart, 1996; Ulrich, *et al.*, 1995).

Huselid, *et al.*, (1997) conducted an elaborate study on 293 firms in the US to evaluate the impact of human resource managers' professional/technical competencies on HR practices and the latter's impact on organisational performance. Results of the study suggest that consistent with the resource-based view of the firm, there exist a significant relationship between SHRM practices and firm performance. They found that: (1) HR related competencies and, to a lesser extent, business-related competencies increase the extent of effective implementation of SHRM practices and; (2) consistent with recent studies linking HRM activities and firm performance (Arthur, 1994; Cutcher-Gershenfeld, 1991; Huselid, 1995; Huselid and Becker, 1996; MacDuffie, 1995), the study support the argument that investments in human resources are a potential source of competitive advantage. Recent reviews of theoretical and empirical literature (Juhary Ali and Bawa, 1999; Irwin, *et al.*, 1998; Jackson and Schuler, 1995) suggest that a variety of factors affect the relationship between HRM and firm performance. These factors include firm size, technology and union coverage.

The influence of *firm size* on HRM practices is fully documented in theoretical and empirical studies. For example, institutional theory suggests that larger organisations should adopt more sophisticated and socially responsive HRM practices because they are more visible and are under more pressure to gain legitimacy. Many empirical studies show that firm size is an important variable influencing HRM practices (Ng and Maki, 1993; Wagar, 1998). There are emerging evidences that HR practices may differ in organisations depending on the *level of technological sophistication* in terms of training, performance appraisal and reward systems.

FRAMEWORK AND PROPOSITIONS

From the discussions so far, the following issues emerge: (1) That there appears to be a significant relationship between strategic HRM practices and firm performance (low employee turnover, high productivity and high profitability (Huselid, *et al.*, 1997); (2) It is also clear that there exist low incidence of implementing SHRM practices relative to technical HRM practices (Huselid, *et al.*, 1997; Wright and McMahan, 1992); (3) Further more although there exists a significant relationship between the extent of both HR professional and business-related managerial competencies and the incidence of implementing HRM practices, organisations have achieved higher levels of HR professional competencies relative to business-related competencies; (4) Finally, environmental context variables like firm size, technology and union status affect the extent of implementing HRM practices (Jackson and Schuler, 1995; Snell and Dean, 1992; Wagar, 1998). The relationships discussed above are presented in the figure below and relevant propositions derived. This theoretical framework is in keeping with the thinking of a number of authors including Delery and Doty (1996), Huselid, *et al.* (1997), Jackson and Schuler (1995) and Wright and McMahan (1992).

Diagram I

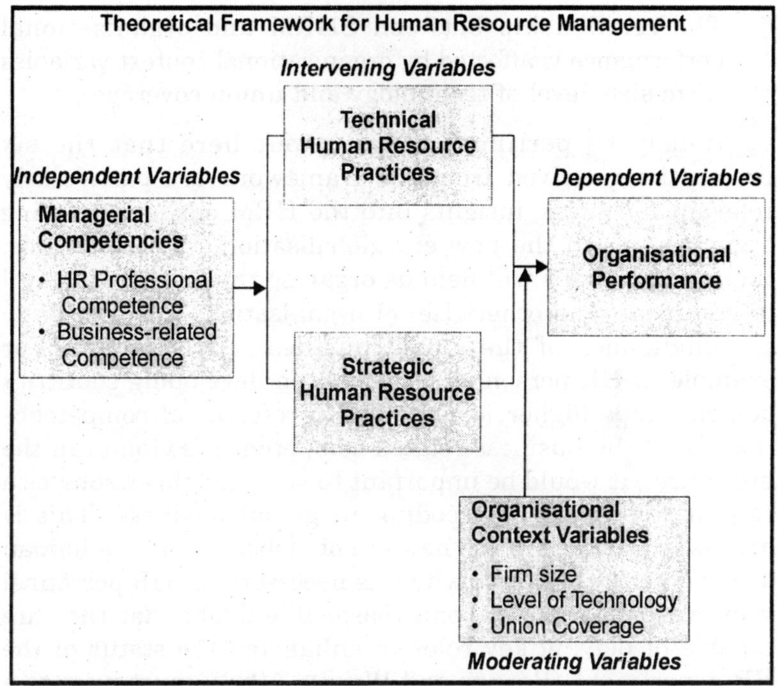

The following testable propositions are derived from the framework above:

1. Human resource managers may have achieved higher levels of HR professional competencies and lower levels of business related competencies;
2. The incidence of implementing strategic HR practices is lower in organisations especially in the developing countries;
3. Both HR professional competence and knowledge of the business (business related competence) significantly contribute to the extent of implementing SHRM Practices;
4. Managerial competencies are significantly related to organisational performance;

5. The extent of implementing SHRM practices contribute significantly to firm level outcomes;
6. The relationship between SHRM and organisational performance is affected by organisational context variables (firm size, level of technology and union coverage).

It may be pertinent to point out here that the six propositions derived from the framework are particularly relevant for giving insights into the HRM challenges facing organisations in the new era globalisation. In other words, these propositions will help us organise thought on the level of readiness (and otherwise) of organisations in response to the challenges of the global business environment. For example, if HR personnel especially in developing countries demonstrates higher levels of HR professional competence relative to the business-related competence (as found in the literature), it would be important to set right this wrong as a stepping stone for succeeding in global business. This is because to succeed in the new era of globalisation, the human factor is central. That is why it is necessary for HR personnel to prove themselves beyond reasonable doubt that they are capable of playing key roles in enhancing the status of the HR department (Barney and Wright, 1988), must possess a thorough understanding of business (Noe, *et al.*, 1997) and also act as important influences in the level of integration between HR management and organisational strategy (Golden and Ramanujam, 1985; Ropo, 1993).

CONCLUSION

This paper set out as a contribution to the current discourse on the interaction of globalisation and business performance especially with a flavour of the challenges from the perspectives of developing countries such as Malaysia and Nigeria. This paper presents a framework for Strategic Human Resource Management as a response to prepare organisations for the challenges of globalisation. It has been observed that by and large organisations have achieved relatively low levels of effectiveness in implementing Strategic

Human Resource Management (SHRM) practices (Huselid, *et al.*, 1997). If the propositions outlined above are supported, then the real challenge for organisations in the era of globalisation is to pay particular emphasis to strengthening their human resources by upgrading the relevant competencies.

As governments and corporate bodies brace up for the new millennium characterised by an ever-increasing global challenge, developing countries have no choice but to develop and continuously upgrade the human resource and business competencies of their workforce. In the case of developing countries, distinct competencies are important to deal with not only the HR issues but also others including partnerships in economic recovery especially in South East Asia, dealing with the "big boys", the fund managers, concerns over possibility of fraud in E-commerce with fast spread of Information Technology and last but not least, implementing prescriptions for recovery and growth taking into consideration the development agenda and unique circumstances of individual countries. Addressing these issues is a necessary step towards facing the challenges of globalisation into the next millennium.

REFERENCES

1. Abowd, J.M. 1990. Does Performance-based Compensation Affect Corporate Performance? *Industrial and Labor Relations Review,* 43: 52-73.

2. Arthur, J.B. 1994. Effects of Human Resource Systems on Manufacturing Performance and Turnover. *Academy of Management Journal,* 37: 670-687.

3. Barney, J. 1991. Firm Resources and Sustained Competitive Advantage. *Journal of Management,* 17: 99-120.

4. Barney, J.B. and Wright, P.M. 1988. On Becoming a Strategic Partner: The Role of Human Resources in Gaining Competitive Advantage. *Human Resource Management,* 37(1): 31-46.

9

Total Quality Management
A Continuous Improvement Process

Balakrushna Panigrahy[♣]
Rabi Narayan Misra[♠]
Satyabrata Dash[♥]

INTRODUCTION

TQM is the way of managing for the future, and is far wider in its application than just assuring product or service quality—it is a way of managing people and business processes to ensure complete customer satisfaction at every stage, internally and externally. TQM, combined with effective leadership, results in an organisation doing the right things right, first time. The core of TQM is the customer-supplier interfaces, both externally and internally, and at each interface lie a number of processes. This core must be surrounded by commitment to quality, communication of the quality message, and recognition of the need to change the culture of the organisation to create total quality. These are

♣ Mr. Balakrushna Panigrahy, MBA Final Year, P.G.C.M.S., S.M.I.T., Berhampur.

♠ Dr. Rabi Narayan Misra, Professor, P.G.C.M.S., S.M.I.T., Berhampur.

♥ Dr. Satyabrata Dash, Lecturer, P.G.C.M.S., S.M.I.T., Berhampur.

the foundations of TQM, and they are supported by the key management functions of people, processes and systems in the organisation. This section discusses each of these elements that, together, can make a total quality organisation. Other sections explain people, processes and systems in greater detail, all having the essential themes of commitment, culture and communication running through them.

To be competitive in today's market, it is essential for construction companies to provide more consistent quality and value to their owners/customers. Now is the time to place behind us the old adversarial approach to managing construction work. It is time to develop better and more direct relationships with our owners/customers, to initiate more teamwork at the jobsite, and to produce better quality work. Such goals demand that a continuous improvement (CI) process be established within the company in order to provide quality management. Ancient Greeks referred to the concept of continuous improvement as well as the Chinese. Recently CI has been referred to as Total Quality Management (TQM). Whichever name is preferred; the concept must be understood and applied to a firm's operations. Meeting owner/customer requirements (providing customer satisfaction) is a primary objective of quality management, and contractors who are the suppliers of construction services must address owner/customer requirements if they are to succeed. The construction industry exists to provide a service to its owners/customers who are becoming more demanding and are seeking higher quality, better value, and lower costs. These owner/customer requirements mirror the economic pressures they face in their own businesses. Implementing total quality management/continuous improvement in managing everyday construction activities is relevant to all those who participate in and contribute to the construction process. TQM is a management philosophy, a paradigm, a continuous improvement approach to doing business through a new management model. The TQM philosophy evolved from the continuous improvement philosophy with a focus on quality as the main dimension of business. Under TQM, emphasising the quality of the product or service predominates. TQM expands beyond statistical process control to embrace a wider scope of management activities of how we manage people and organisations by focussing on the entire process, not just simple measurements.

TQM is a comprehensive management system which:

- Focusses on meeting owners'/customers' needs by providing quality services at a cost that provides value to the owners/customers;
- Is driven by the quest for continuous improvement in all operations;
- Recognises that everyone in the organisation has owners/customers who are either internal or external;
- Views an organisation as an internal system with a common aim rather than as individual departments acting to maximise their own performances;
- Focusses on the way tasks are accomplished rather than simply what tasks are accomplished;
- Emphasises teamwork and a high level of participation by all employees presented here are universal total quality management beliefs;
- Owner/customer satisfaction is the measure of quality;
- Everyone has owners/customers; everyone is an owner/customer;
- Quality improvement must be continuous;
- Analysing the processes used to create products and services is key to quality improvement;
- Measurement, a skilled use of analytical tools, and employee involvement are critical sources of quality improvement ideas and innovations;

- ❖ Sustained total quality management is not possible without active, visible, consistent, and enabling leadership by managers at all levels;
- ❖ If we do not continuously improve the quality of products and services that we provide our owners/ customers, someone else will motivate towards other products.

Scope and Objective of the Study

Human Resource Management (HRM) plays an important role after globalisation. The purpose of the study is to know the adoption of the total quality management in the different organisations. TQM has played an important role which need due considerations. For this purpose we have taken the secondary datas by referring various journals, books, magazines, Internets and other sources. So, all the limitations of the secondary data are available in the study.

The Building Blocks of TQM

Everything we do is a process, which is the transformation of a set of inputs, which can include action, methods and operations, into the desired outputs, which satisfy the customers' needs and expectations. In each area or function within an organisation there will be many processes taking place, and each can be analysed by an examination of the inputs and outputs to determine the action necessary to improve quality. In every organisation there are some very large processes, which are groups of smaller processes, called key or core business processes. These must be carried out well if an organisation is to achieve its mission and objectives. The section on processes discusses processes and how to improve them, and implementation covers how to prioritise and select the right process for improvement (Zeithaml and Bitner, 2003).

The only point at which true responsibility for performance and quality can lie is with the people who actually do the job or carry out the process, each of which has one or several suppliers and customers. An efficient and effective way to tackle process or quality improvement is through teamwork. However, people will not engage in improvement activities without commitment and recognition from the organisation's leaders, a climate for improvement and a strategy that is implemented thoughtfully and effectively. The section on people expands on these issues, covering roles within teams, team selection and development and models for successful teamwork.

An appropriate documented Quality Management System will help an organisation not only achieve the objectives set out in its policy and strategy, but also, and equally importantly, sustain and build upon them. It is imperative that the leaders take responsibility for the adoption and documentation of an appropriate management system in their organisation if they are serious about the quality journey. The systems section discusses the benefits of having such a system, how to set one up and successfully implement it.

Once the strategic direction for the organisation's quality journey has been set, it needs performance measures: to monitor and control the journey, and to ensure the desired level of performance is being achieved and sustained. They can, and should be, established at all levels in the organisation, ideally being cascaded down and most effectively undertaken as team activities and this is discussed in the section on performance.

Characteristics of Successful TQM Companies

The construction industry has arrived late to TQM, probably due to the tendency to easily brush aside anything in management that is new, or to dismiss TQM as a fad. Continuous improvement is not a fad but a necessary part of management's obligation to properly run its company. Gone are the boom days when quality did not matter due to the volume of work available and the ease of obtaining work. The attitude of construction managers and contractors was simply to add it to the bill, because the owner will pay for it.

In other words, in those boom days cost plus profit equaled price. Now, however, the new attitude is price minus cost equals profit. Owners are now demanding higher quality work, and at a lower cost. In attempting to keep pace with the new attitude, a quality management system that helps keeps costs down is well worth implementing. The characteristics that are common to companies that successfully implement TQM in their daily operations are listed here (Zeithaml and Bitner, 2003):

- Strive for owner/customer satisfaction and employee satisfaction;
- Strive for accident-free jobsites;
- Recognise that the owner/customer provides the revenue while the employees are responsible for the profit;
- Recognise the need for measurement and fact-based decision making;
- Arrange for employees to become involved in helping the company improve;
- Train extensively;
- Work hard at improving communication inside and outside the company;
- Use teams of employees to improve processes;
- Place a strong emphasis on the right kind of leadership, and provide supervisors with a significant amount of leadership training;
- Involve subcontractors and suppliers, requiring them to adopt TQM;
- Strive for continuous improvement.

The quality principles that successful TQM companies recognise and attempt to continually incorporate into their actions are the following (Zeithaml and Bitner, 2003):

- People will produce quality goods and services when the meaning of quality is expressed daily in their relations with their work, colleagues, and organisation;
- Inspection of the process is as important as inspection of the product. Quality improvement can be achieved by the workers closest to the process;
- Each system with a certain degree of complexity has a probability of variation, which can be understood by scientific methods;
- Workers work in the system to improve the system, managers work on the system to improve the system;
- Total quality management is a strategic choice made by top management, and must be consistently translated into guidelines provided to the whole organisation;
- Envision what you desire to be as an organisation, but start working from where you actually are;
- Studies have indicated that people like working on a quality-managed jobsite especially due to the cleaner site and safer place to work;
- Accept the responsibility for quality;
- Establish datum for measurement;
- Use the principle of get it right, the first time, every time;
- Understand that quality is a journey, not a destination. It consists of steps that form a process that is continuous.

The reasons to begin establishing quality improvement processes now are several. Study the various areas below to determine which would affect your company in a positive way. It is believed that all of the following would be of great benefit. Cost reasons are discussed at the end of this section, under.

For Management/For Employee

- Provides an invaluable problem-solving tool for managers and supervisors to use;
- Dispels negative attitudes;
- Management becomes more aware of problems that affect the individual's work environment;
- Employees gain a sense of participation;
- Increases efficiency and productivity;
- Reduces turnover rate, tardiness, costs, errors, and scrap and rework;
- Improves communications within and among all departments;
- Develops management skills that were never taught, or are long forgotten due to lack of application;
- Develops overall company awareness and company unity;
- Rearranges priorities which once seemed locked in place;
- Builds loyalty to the company;
- Reveals training requirements in all departments;
- Lessens the number of defects received from suppliers when they are encouraged to train in quality management;
- Provides opportunity for personal growth and development (as a result of team training activities) and the opportunity to develop and present recommendations;
- Increases innovation (through a greater variety of approaches and perspectives) for solving problems, removing fear of failure;

- ❖ Employees use their knowledge and skills to generate data-driven recommendations that will lead for decision-making;
- ❖ Encourages decision-making at the most appropriate level;
- ❖ increases motivation and acceptance of new ideas;
- ❖ Increases job satisfaction (as a result of the opportunity to participate in and have influence over work);
- ❖ Recognises employees for their knowledge, skills, and contribution toward improvement;
- ❖ Develops mutual respect among employees, management and customers promotes teamwork.

In the study by Cardy and his associates (1995) they assert that "the quality approach emphasises the importance of striving to avoid committing errors in the first place." Moreover, workers are given the tools and responsibility for assessing the quality of their own work. As such, quality approach decentralises the traditional inspection function and integrates it into the work process itself. The assumption that errors are largely due to system factors rather than worker characteristics is another important characteristic of the quality approach. Additionally, Cardy (1998) argues that since system factors are assumed to be the major determinant of performance variability, this assumption can be thought of as underlying the prevention emphasis. Specifically, if errors are to be avoided, the most important means for doing this is a focus on the system, not on individual workers. In sum, A Cardy states that "performance is mainly a function of system factors and improvement in this performance thus requires improvement in the system."

Employee or staff appraisal can be defined as the process whereby current performance in a job is observed and discussed for the purpose of adding to that level of performance (Randell, 1994). Even though this is a simple definition of an every day managerial activity it is a controversial topic. The literature abounds with different analyses and conclusions that arise from how the process of employee performance measurement is viewed and how it is seen to fit with business strategy, personnel policy and individual managerial philosophies. A brief review of the literature indicates that performance appraisal has been lamented by many researchers as an unwelcome and difficult task for a variety of reasons i.e. a tool for managerial control, focus on the past, individual responsibility for performance, error and bias. Even though the role of evaluation may be uncomfortable for many, Cardy (1998) asserts that 'judgments of performance are needed if performance contingent decisions, ranging from termination to pay increase and promotion, are to have any sort of rational basis.' The remainder of this section examines the conflicts between traditional and quality approaches to performance appraisal in order to find out the characteristics of performance appraisal that could maximise the effectiveness of appraisal in a quality-driven context.

CONCLUSION

TQM played a significant role to the organisation after globalisation. The HRM and TQM played a significant role for development of Industries. Price is not considering in the modern era, but the quality of the product is need due consideration not only for the organisation but also for the buyers and the market researchers who are dealing with the study of market.

Continuous improvement of the product will accumulate the management process by gearing up the profits of the Organisation. It increase not only the production of the organisation but also the efficiency of staffs those who are working in the organisation.

REFERENCE

1. Cardy R.L. and Dobbins G.H. (1996), 'Human Resource Management in a Total Quality Management environment:

Shifting from a Traditional to a TQHRM Approach', *Journal of Quality Management,* Vol. 1, pp. 5-20.

2. Cardy R.L. (1998), 'Performance Appraisal in a Quality Context: A New Look at an Old Problem'. In Smither J. W. (ed), *Performance Appraisal: State of the Art in Practice;* San Francisco: Jossey-Bass Publishers.
3. Randell G. (1994), 'Employee Appraisal'. In Sisson K. (ed), *'Personnel Management: A Comprehensive Guide to Theory and Practice in Britain';* Oxford: Blackwell Publishers Ltd.
4. Zeithaml, V.A. and Bitner, M.J., Service Marketing (2003), 3rd Edition, pp. 70-75.

10

Changing Strategies in HRM
Performance Appraisal System in IRE Ltd.

Krishnamaya Dev[♣]
Rabi. N. Misra[♠]

INTRODUCTION

Globalisation represents the structural making of the world characterised by the free flow of technology and human resources across national boundaries new boundaries as well as the spread of information technology (IT) and mass media presenting an ever changing and competitive business environment. Since the human factor is the key in the new era of globalisation, the primary objective is to present a conceptual framework for effective management of human resources as a response to the growing interaction of globalisation and business performance.

That in order to manage employees for competitive edge in a period of globalisation human resource personnel must posses competitiveness relevant for implementing such strategic HRM policies and practices.

♣ Miss Krishnamaya Dev is a Research Scholar, MBA Student.

♠ Dr. Rabi. N. Misra, Professor, MBA, PGCMS, SMIT, Ankushpur.

Guided by theoretical perspectives such as firms resource based theory of competitive advantage and empirical evidence, this paper develop propositions, draws implications for the strategic management of human resources to prepare organisations for the challenges of globalisation.

Since the human factor is one of the key issues in the new era of globalisation, the primary objective, therefore is to present a conceptual framework for strategic management of human resources as a response to the growing interaction of globalisation and business performance.

The central arguments made are:

- ❖ That a great deal of evidence suggest that, changes taking place in global business environment often, are not accompanied by complementary changes in human resource management practices leading to a situation whereby the failure of some firms is due to the mismanagement of people rather than to problems with technical systems;
- ❖ This is because organisations have achieved relatively low levels of effectiveness in implementing strategic human resource management (SHRM) practices;
- ❖ This is particularly the case in emerging economies of South East Asia like Malaysia and other developing countries like Nigeria that are exposed to the challenges and opportunities of globalisation;
- ❖ In order to manage employees for competitive edge in a period of globalisation, human resource personnel must posses competencies relevant for effective implementation of such strategic HRM policies and practices.

This paper develops competency based research framework and draws implications for the strategic management of human resources to prepare organisations for the challenges of globalisation.

The coming of 21st century, globalisation poses distinctive challenges to businesses especially those operating across national boundaries as multinational or global enterprise. Global business is characterised by the free flow of human and financial resources especially in the developed economies of European Union (EU), the North American Free Trade Agreement (NAFTA), other regional groupings such as the Association of South East Asian Nations (ASEAN), the Economic Community of West African States (ECOWAS). The South African Development Community etc. These developments are opening up of new markets in a way that has never has been seen before. This accentuates the need to manage human resources effectively to gain competitive advantage in the global market place.

To achieve this, organisations require an understanding of the factors that can determine the effectiveness of various HR practices and approaches. A number of factors that effect HRM in global markets are: (1) Culture; (2) Economic System; (3) Political System—the legal framework; and (4) Human Capital. Consistent with the scope of this paper, only one dimension is treated i.e. Human Capital (the skills, capabilities or competencies of the work for Human Resource Development played an important role for the growth and development of the organisation. Unless importance has been given on the growth of human capital, an organisation will not achieve its goal. So the Indian Rate Earth has taken many steps on manpower planning like recruitment, training and performance appraisal system. In this study an attempt has been taken regarding the performance appraisal system, which measure the quality, excellency, faithfulness, job performance and job satisfaction of an employee, so that they will be promoted to next higher job.

The IRE Ltd measures the performance appraisal of employees once in a year. For this purpose they have taken the executive personnel mostly officers. The Human Resource (HR) Department of the IRE send the assessment report of an employee taking into consideration the Performance

Appraisal to the Head, through Chief General Manager for due consideration.

SCOPE AND OBJECTIVES OF THE STUDY

In this article we have highlighted regarding the performance appraisal system of IRE Ltd of Chatrapur, Ganjam after Globalisation. For this purpose all published datas are taken into consideration, so all limitations of secondary data are found in this study.

ABOUT IRE LTD

Before discussing about the performance appraisal system, let us know something about the organisation of Indian Rare Earth Ltd.

Indian Rare Earth Ltd is a central public sector undertaking under the administrative control of the Department of Atomic Energy, Govt of India. The company is engaged in the mining of beach sand minerals in the coastal areas for processing of beach sand minerals such as ilmenite, sillimanite, rutile , zircon and monazite.

Since incorporation of the company at Mumbai in 1950 the company has grown steadily during the past 50 years and the sales turnover of the company as 300(Crores) approx. With several diversification plans in progress, including modernisation of existing plants and machinery, the company is poised for furthur growth with a significant earning of valuable foreign exchange for the nation. IREL caters to international markets viz USA, UK, France, Germany, Norway, Japan, China etc even under severe global competition.

Over 32 export awards that IRE has won bear eloquent testimony to its consistent export performance. Over the decade, IRE has built up a corporate image in the world market as a reliable supplier of beach sand minerals and rare earth compound. The ISO 9002 Certification by all operating unit of IRE bear furthur testimony to the commitment of the company for quality and customer satisfaction.

The company's pride lies in its harmonious cordial relationship with employees for several years. The production plants of IREL have adopted higher level of safety standards along with environment friendly techniques to exploit the abundantly available minerals from the beaches of eastern and western parts of Indian peninsula.

The management of the company is entrusted with a group of highly qualified experienced directors drawn from different fields such as technical, marketing, finance and R&D and mining as per its operations. Management of the company has formulated the mission statement for realising of there making IREL, a leading supplier of beach sand minerals from Asia.

IREL being established as rare earths company, beach sand minerals business has continued to be the main stay of IREL, and is expected to remain so. In the current changing environment of liberalisation which has promoted global participation and entry of private entrepreneurs into the field of beach sand minerals, IREL management is adopting dynamic and innovative policies to maintain its lead in the world market.

PERFORMANCE APPRAISAL OF THE CONCEPT IN GENERAL

Performance appraisal system is practised in almost every organisation. Performance Appraisals are done for evaluating performance of employees or for developing them. They are two types:

1. Informing the employee where he stands using the data for personal pay promotions etc;
2. Developmental objectives focus on finding individual and organisational strengths and weaknesses. Developing superior subordinate relationships, offering counselling to develop skill and maximum potential of the employee. Thus it serves several useful purposes such as:
   - ❖ Compensation decisions;

- ❖ Promotion decisions;
- ❖ Training and development programmes;
- ❖ Feedback to know how well he is doing his job;
- ❖ Personal development of employees and how they contribute to the betterment and improvement of the organisations for maximum efficiency and output.

Performance Appraisal Systems are designed to improve performance. They cover areas like:

1. Define performance;
2. Fecilitate performance;
3. Encourage performance;
4. Management by objectives.

The appraisal system are used for a variety of development and administrative purposes. Appraisals can be done either informally or systematically. Systematic appraisals are usually done annually. Appraisals can be done by superiors, peers, subordinates, teams, outsiders or a combination of raters can do appraisals. Employees can also carry self appraisals. Mainly 3 types of appraisal method are used:

1. Individual Evaluation Method;
2. Multiperson Evaluation Method and other methods including HRA, assessment centre;
3. 360-degree feedback etc.

Under Individual Evaluation Method of merit rating, employees are evaluated one at a time without concerning them with other employees in the organisation. They include i.e.:

(a) Confidential report prepared at the end of the year by the employees of immediate superior. This method is followed by the Government;

(b) Easy evaluation is done by a rater who expresses the story, and weak points of the employee,

employers understanding of the companys programme, policies and objectives. The employees general planning , organising and controlling ability. Attitudes 'and perceptions of the employee in general. It is highly subjective and may not be impartial, as some evaluators have poor writing skill and time consuming. Thus from the firms point of view it becomes costly and time consuming.

In Multiperson Evaluation Technique the following methods are used:

(a) *Ranking Method:* Here the ranking of one person against anathor in a working group;

(b) *Paired Comparison Method:* Where each worker is compared with all other employees;

(c) *Forced Distiribution Method:* Under this system the rater is asked to appraise according to predetermined distribution scale;

(d) *Group Appraisal:* Under, this a group of appraisers evaluate employees performance;

(e) *Human Resource Accounting:* Measures, in financial terms the effectiveness of personal management and the use of people in a management. The positive performance can be measured in terms of percentage excess of employee contribution compared to cost of employee. This method becomes very expensive because HRA experts do it;

Under 360 Degree feedback system, collects feedback from multiple sources. In practice 360-degree system becomes a sensitive issue. It may fail to deliver results if not implemented properly.

Management by Objectives or *The MBO Method*: MBO Method requires the manage to set specific measurable goals with each employee and periodically discuss the letters progress towards these goals. This technique emphasises participatively set goals that are tangible, verifiable and measurable. MBO emphasises attention on what must be accomplished rather than how it is accomplished. It is a goal setting appraisal programme involving six steps:

1. ***Set Organisational goals:*** Establish an organisational plan for next year and set company goals;
2. ***Set departmental goals:*** Departments take the broader company goals and with their superiors jointly set goals for the department;
3. ***Discuss departmental goals:*** The department goals are discussed in a departmental meeting with subordinates. The heads require the subordinates to set their own goals focussing on what they can do to achieve the departmental goals;
4. ***Define expected results:*** The department heads and subordinates agree on a set participatory, set short term and individual targets;
5. ***Performance Reviews:*** Here the heads compare each employee's actual and targeted performance, periodically and annually, with the intention to identify and solve performance problems and to assess and reward ones overall contribution to the organisation. Employees are evaluated on their performance results, hence MBO is known as result based performance appraisal system;
6. ***Provide feedback:*** Here both parties evaluate progress made in achieving goals, and rectify past mistakes of the employee, and enable him to meet targets in future, focussing attention on his strengths.

The MBO Method is time consuming to set verifiable goals at all levels of an organisation. In the race to define everything rigidly, some qualitative aspects might be ignored. Often goals may be set at frustatingly high level ignoring the subordinates wish to have at more comfortable levels. At time, short term goals take precedence over long term goals. To overcome these problems, allow managers at all levels, to explain coordinate and guide the programme in a persuasive, democratic way. The jointly set targets must be .fair and attainable. Both superiors and subordinates should be taught to set realistic goals and be familiarise with the results for which they are finally held responsible.

PERRFORMANCE APPRAISAL PRACTICES IN INDIA

There are three different approaches for carrying out appraisals:

1. Absolute standards, where employees performance is measured against some established standards. The subjects are not compared with any other person;
2. *Interpersonal effectiveness:* This includes directedness, negotiating power, personal influence and verbal behaviour;
3. *Operational effectiveness:* This includes result orientation, individual effectiveness and stability;
4. *Achievement motivation:* This includes drive, professional ambition, innovativeness and stability. The potential of an employee is measured along their dimensions on a five point scale.

Philips lays down a fast track career growth plan for the star performers in 5 to 10 year plan. Companies like Glaxo and Cadbury have similar processes in place of similar star performers from the employee ranks and exploit their potential fully using rewards and incentive schemes to maximum good effect.

CHALLENGES IN PERFORMANCE MANAGEMENT

In present day organisations, the twin principles of motivating are common at all levels, acknowledge unique contributions and alleviate personal concerns that impact professional competence.

To get the best out of people the C.E.O's should:

1. Create a cultural excellence that motivates employees at all levels;
2. Match organisational objectives with individual aspiration;
3. Equip people with requisite skills to discharge their duties well;
4. Clear growth path for talented employees;
5. Provide new challenges to rejuvenate flatting concerns;
6. Empower employees to take decisions without fear or failings,
7. Encourage teamwork and team spirit and open communication

Appraisals should be carried out in objective manner, scrupulously following the criteria laid down for this purpose. When appraisals take a positive route, several problems arise, such as rating errors, poor forms, and lack of rater preparedness, ineffective organisational policies and practices.

To improve reliability and validity of ratings it is essential to train raters. For this a variety of suggestions are advanced by H.R. Professionals to overcome the problems. Recent approaches to performance management have involved more parties in the whole process of evaluation including subordinates, peers, customers etc.

Giving and receiving feedback is not an easy task. If done properly, both organisation and employee will immensely benefit from such an exercise.

PERFORMANCE APPRAISAL SYSTEM OF IRE LTD

Performance Appraisal is systematic evaluation of current and potential abilities expected. Performance appraisal (PA) is termed as merit rating and is the process of communicating an employee about his job performance. It is method of systematic, periodic and impartial rating of ones excellence in matters concerning to his present job and his future potentialities. It is also the process of evaluating the performance and qualification of the job for which he is employed, for the purpose of administration including placement, selection for promotion. Providing financial rewards and other actions, which require differential treatment among the members of the group as distinguished from action affecting all members equally. The ultimate goal of theirs is to place the right people in the right job to achieve organisational excellence.

GENERAL

In general the performance of the organisation depends on the performance of its employees. In this direction management of IREL has adopted a revised system of performance appraisal which requires the setting of Key Result Areas by the Reporting Officer in consultation with the Appraisee. The performance of the officers is assessed annually through performance appraisal and is an essential input for assessment of officers of the company for their career progression as well as for identification of their needs.

USED

1. P.A is used to identify the current job knowledge in the area in which one is functioning;
2. To identify the strengths and weaknesses of an officer performing in a job;
3. To identify training needs.

PURPOSE

(a) The primary purpose is to assess the officers performance to check whether he has attuned with the organisation and whether the officer has role clarity and renders services as expected of him or her;

(b) The second goal of the system is performance enhancement consequent to performance assessment. The basic function in improving ones performance is to give him a timely and proper feedback on his performance communication of

adverse entries to the officer is part of this feedback system and hence is very much necessary, so that the officer becomes aware of the specific points on which he is required to improve upon;

(*c*) The third goal of the system is to generate reliable data for training or such other developmental efforts and to offer assistance to the officer for their improvement;

(*d*) P.A is required to be used at the time of consideration of the cases of the officer for—

A. Promotion;

B. Confirmation;

C. Transfer;

D. Deputation including deputation abroad;

E. Review for retention in service;

F. Determining training needs for further improvement in perforfmance.

(*e*) Key Result Areas (KRAs) are set in mutual consultation with the appraise by the reporting officer and will be reviewed during mid term. The KRAs will be aligned with functional areas.

PERFORMANCE APPRAISAL REPORTS

Performance Appraisal reports have been designed by the company as tool for setting, monitoring and evaluation of performance of the officer vis-a-vis Key Result Areas that will be assigned to every officer. Therefore Key Result Areas will be set for each officer in such a manner that they are commensurate with the position occupied by him in the hierarchy of the unit. To ensure that the KRAs are fixed in such a manner that they are achievable within the realistic measures of Time and Targets, mutual setting of KRAs well in time is a prime requirement of our performance appraisal system.

A. PERFORMANCE FACTOR

1. Job Knowledge
2. Job Planning
3. Job Execution
4. Problem Locating
5. Human Relation
6. Information Sharing/Knowledge

B. POTENTIAL FACTOR

1. Initiatives
2. Innovativeness
3. Keeping abstract and latent development
4. Ability to listen
5. Development of subordinates etc.

OBJECTIVES OF KRAs

KRAs stand for Key Result Areas. Identification of KRAs for each officer is the most essential step to ensure Management By Objectives (MBO). KRAs are parameters for performance setting, performance monitoring, and performance evaluation both during mid term of financial year and at the end of financial year, to ensure that all the department are moving ahead in the right direction and in the right pace, as per objectives set by the company and the unit.

In IRE Ltd, Matikhalo, performance appraisal of employees is done once in a year. There are two categories of employees, they are officers and workmen. The workmen are covered under Trade Union Act and protected.

The officers performance appraisal is done in a period of one financial year. All the officers are issued with a Key Resource Area format. The key resource area is identified by all the officers with due weightage after consultation and mutual agreement with reporting officer. After 6 months the performance of activity of the officer is analysed by reporting officer. In case of any deviation it is rectified and suitable action is taken. At the end of the year the reporting officer examines and evaluates the performance. The appraisal form is forwarded to the reviewing officer he who in turn reviews and evaluates the performance.

The reviewing officer forwards the form with all his remarks to the unit head. The format gives the strength and weaknesses of the concerned employee. This format helps during departmental promotion and placement of employees. Departmental committee promotes all the officers after the interview.

While promotion to next higher rank the departmental promotion committee reviews the performance in an interview, performance in key resource area and managerial skill of the reporting officer. 50 per cent of weightage is provided to the performance in the interview. Out of balance 50 per cent point 3 weightage is provided to the performance in KRA. A weightage of point 4 is provided to the performance factor and weightage of point 3 is provided to potential factor.

In case of senior officers the weightage of point 3 is provided for performance factor and point 4 potential factor. There are 10 grades.

Allocation of Weights

Level	*KRAs*	*Performance Factor*	*Potential Factor*	*Total*
Officers to Managers	0.3	0.4	0.3	1.00
Senior Manager And Above	0.3	0.3	0.4	1.00

Determination of Overall Grade

Score	*Rating*	*Overall Grade*
9.5 & Above	Outstanding	A+
9 to 9.49	Excellent	A
8 to 8.99	Very Good	A–
7 to 7.99	Good	B+
6 to 6.99	Above Average	B
5 to 5.99	Average	B–
4 to 4.99	Below Average	C
3 to 3.99	Fair	C–
2 to 2.99	Poor	D
Below 2	Very Poor	E

For the workmen at the time of work the concerned supervisors take the stock of the performance and keeps records of its performance. In case of any adverse remark and poor performance and indiscipline he reports the matter to the concerned HOD, and the concerned authority, after seeing the gravity of the matter reports to Human Resource Management Department, HRM Dept conducts a departmental enquiry. In the enquiry natural justice is given by receiving the opinion of the concerned employee.

Based on enquiry report suitable disciplinary action is taken against the concerned employee, and promotion is made on time scale provided there is no adverse remark during the period.

CONCLUSION

Employees appraisal is important for manpower development because it reveals strengths and weaknesses of an employee. And accordingly development plans can be prepared for each employee. Development of a person on his own performance appraisal leads to improved job performance. The appraisal employee qualifies for himself for higher responsibility, more rewarding assignment and promotion. The appraisal programmes directed towards the actual performance of an employee on his present job as well as potential for promotion to a higher level position.

The performance appraisal both in case of executives and non executives is neither formalised in the unit nor the corporate office provides explicit rules for this purpose. It is done in an informal basis in order to exercise control and maintain some sort of discipline among the employees. So that , it may help in increasing productivity and goodwill of the organisation.

The performance appraisal system is effectively used in Indian Rare Earths Ltd, Matikhalo (OSCOM) for its entire employee. The evolution report should be changed and it is high time that top management takes firm steps in this direction. The management must be committed to the development of human resource in Indian Rare Earths Ltd, Matikhalo. Investment in terms of management time, training, job enrichment and such programmes become integral part of the management process. A good degree of openness and interpersonal trust in the organisation is utmost necessity. They must be entrusted in creating more open, collaborating and mutually trusting climate in the whole organisation.

Above all the Indian Rare Earths Ltd, Matikhalo top management must believe that development of human resource will contribute to its effectiveness, productivity and ultimately performance. All this will make the performance appraisal system and top management levels role more effective in Indian Rare Earths Ltd. Matikhalo (O).

An obvious question at this juncture is: How can organisations effectively adopt, implement and maximise HRM practices for valued firm level outcomes ? That is how can firms increase the probability that they will adopt and then effectively implement appropriate HRM practices. Insuring that members of the HRM personnel have the appropriate human capital or competencies has been suggested as one way to increase the likelihood of effective implementation of HRM practices.

As Governments and corporate bodies brace up for the new millennium characterised by the ever increasing global challenge, developing countries have no choice but to develop and continuously upgrade the human resource and business competencies of their workforce. In the case of developing countries, distinct competence are important to deal not only the HR issues but also including partnerships in economic recovery especially in South East Asia, dealing with the "big boys", the fund managers, concerns over possibility of fraud in E-Commerce with fast spread of Information Technology and last but not least, implementing prescriptions for recovery and growth, taking into consideration the development agenda and unique circumstances of individual countries. Addressing these issues is a necessary step towards facing the challenges of globalisation into the next millennium.

Economics of Education and Development

Some Theoretical and Practical Insights with Reference to Orissa

Govinda Chandra Mohankuda♣
B. Eswar Rao Pattnaik♠

INTRODUCTION

The term education is employed by Vedic Scholars to denote "*Tatwamsi Swetaketu*". To Aristotle "Education is the capacity to feel pleasure and pain at the right moment". M.K. Gandhi, 'The Father of the Nation' considers education as a process that draws out of the best in the child and man body, mind and spirit.

Amartya Sen maintains that development centers round enhancement of capabilities of people by enforcing their entitlements to education and health. Of late, the meaning

♣ Mr. Mohankuda, Lecturer in Education, S.B. Science College, Konisi, Ganjam.

♠ B. Eswar Rao Pattnaik, Reader in Economics, S.B.R.G. Women's College, Berhampur.

of development has been broadened to expansion of freedoms and choices that citizens enjoy in a country.

The traditional approach to development has been focus on per capita income as the index of the development of a country. The per capita income criterion looks at the surface and bypasses the depth of the human side of development. The endeavour of U.N.D.P. has culminated in the development of physical quality of life index. The focus now on real per capita income, literacy, accomplishment and longevity of people, while assessing per capita income in economy.

The study assumes pivotal importance because Jean Dreze and Amartya Sen (1997) contend that, being an educated has direct importance to a person's effective freedom. The instrumental role of education is the possibilities of getting a job for making use of economic opportunities. Basic education may facilitate public discussion of social needs.

T. Schultz has floated the idea in his thesis work on education in Chicago school that, investment and education schooling on the job training and migration are contributory factors for economic development. It was only in 1969 that, Dudly Seers broke the growth fetism of development they and has argued that development is the social phenomenon that involves more than increasing per capita income. Recently, Mahbub ul Haq, has focussed on redefinition on economic development Human capital is the quality of human beings in respect of productive work. Schultz emphasised that, labour performs not one but two functions. One is to provide the regular physical labour, Secondly it helps in the process of production and enhances the productivity through application of knowledge and skills.

Overall, the research conducted in the areas of education has been rich, diverse and vibrant. It covered three distinct areas: *(A)* Education development relationship; *(B)* Educational productive function; and *(C)* Financing of education.

The studies on education development relationship stressed on rate of return analysis, simple correlation, production function, estimating residual coefficient of education and simultaneous equations. Some scholars focussed on internal efficiency in education through impact of education on employment and fundamental for others is the contribution of education for GDP. Thanks to the pioneering works of Paul Romer (1986), Robert Lucas (1988), and Richard Barror (1999) the role of education in economic progress has received global attention. Under the magnetic impact of Strumulin's work in Russia and George Psacharopoulos, rate of return to education is estimated with the help of mincerian earning function or discounted life time earnings and costs of education. The rate of return to education has occupied the center stage both in developed and developing countries.

In India the doors for the welcome guest education was opened in the early 1960's with the seminar works of V.K.R.V. Rao, A.M. Nalla Gounden, V.N. Kothari and P.R. Panchamukhi and recently A.K. Sen and P.R. Brahmananda.

APPROACHES TO EDUCATION

Education has many aspects, such as economic, social and cultural (D.C. Mishra, 1989).

NEED FOR INVESTMENT IN EDUCATION

It is plausible to believe that, education and training enhances capabilities of human beings, improve their longevity and life time earning through their positive impact on productivity. Education, undoubtedly is the key to the effective functioning of a person's freedom. It needs recognition that, education, knowledge and skill adds to one's earning capacity, widen the base for job opportunities and renders possible public discussion of social needs.

Education and health seems to be valuable to the freedom of a person in at least five distinct ways:

(i) ***Intrinsic importance:*** Being educated and healthy are valuable achievements in themselves;

(ii) ***Instrumental personal roles:*** A person's education and health can help him or her to do

many things—other than just being educated and healthy that are also valuable. They can, for instance, be important for getting a job and more generally for making use of economic opportunities.

The resulting expansion in incomes and economic means can, in turn, add to a person's freedom to achieve functioning's that he or she values;

(iii) ***Instrumental social roles:*** Greater literacy and basic education can facilitate public discussion of social needs and encourage in forcing collective demands (e.g. for health care and social security); these in turn can help expand the facilitates that the public enjoys. For example, the incidence of child labour is closely connected with non-schooling of children, and the expansion of schooling can the reduce the distressing phenomena of child labour, prevalent in India. Schooling also brings young people in torch with others and thereby broadness their horizons, and this can be particularly important for young girls;

(iv) ***Employment and distributive role:*** Great literacy and educational achievement of disadvantaged groups can increase their ability to resist oppression, to organise politically and to get a fairer deal. The redistributive effects can be important not only between different social groups or households, but also within the family, since there is evidence that better education (particularly female education) contributes to the reduction of gender-based inequalities.

PECULIARITIES OF EDUCATION AND THEORETICAL APPROACHES TO ECONOMICS OF EDUCATION

The English classical economics may add a sharp distinction between capital and labour in development theories accumulation of physical capital has occupied the centre stage of discussion. But thanks to industrial revolution, there has been progress of technology which increased the importance the skill in labour force and the distinction between labour as an original factor of production and capital as a producer factor of production has become unrealistic. The limitation of material capital to quote Dr. D.C. Mishra as an explanation of growth has captured the attention of economists to the concept of human capital as complementary explanation.

Conceptually, capital accumulation includes such diverse elements as: (i) adding to physical capital; (ii) Increasing the health , discipline, skill and education human population; (iii) Moving labour to more productive occupations and localities. And applying existing knowledge or discovering new knowledge to increase the efficiency of the productive process.

While expenditure in education comprises a major component of human capital, contribution of education to development is difficult for quantitative measurement due to peculiar features of such education.

(i) The direct output of educational expenditure is not easily measurable;

(ii) There is a long gestation period in education. There may be an interval of 15 to 20 years between the initial investment and the appearance of the output;

(iii) Educational expenditure is an investment, in so far as, it increases human competence and skill and thus increases productivity and income but it is partly consumption expenditure because it yields utility over time. It is difficult to separate the investment and consumption aspects of educational expenditure, it depends on the use to which the output of educational expenditure is put;

(iv) Educational expenditure is permissive. It creates opportunities for growth of output. It is necessary but not sufficient condition for growth of output;

(v) Last but not the least there is not determinate functional relationship betweens inputs and outputs, mainly, because success depends on complementary measures.

Broadly speaking, economists and social thinkers around the world have visualised three lines of approach to assess the contribution of education, not withstanding its difficulty of quantification of educations, contribution for society. They are:

1. The simple correlation approach;
2. The residual approach; and
3. The rate of return approach.

The simple correlation approach explains growth rate in education in relation to GNP. But the simple correlation approach cannot give an indication as to what growth rate in education is related to how much increase in G.N.P. Therefore, it cannot be used for planning and policy making purpose in developing countries.

The exponents of residual approach ascribes that part of the increase in a country's total output which cannot be explained by measurable factors such as, labour and capital to growth in education and knowledge. This approach may have relevance to be advanced countries of the best. But is hardly applicable to developing countries. The heterogeneity of the elements that go to make up this residual makes it difficult to prescribe any policy for education alone.

THE RATE OF RETURN APPROACH

The rate of return approach seeks to determine the allocation of resources between investment in education and investment in other sectors in economy.

It also serves as a guide with regard to allocation of educational expenditure between different channels of education. Separate rates of returns can be computed for arts and science graduates, as well as, for doctors and engineers. This approach is better than other two approaches but it has its own limitations.

Groups with differing amounts of education differ systematically in terms of other attributes which may influence relative earnings and may not reflect the differences in marginal productivity. It is possible to state that, education, earning and endowment and individual motivation are interrelated and it is difficult to isolate the pure effects of education on earnings. The returns principles does not reflect the external or indirect benefit generated by education which may be sizeable in a developing country.

To study the impact of changes, comparisons has been made between two periods, the pre-green revolution period covering years 1950-51 to 1964-65 and the post-green revolution period covering period 1964-65 to 1984-85 are given in Table 11.1.

Table 11.1: Compound Growth Rate of G.N.P. and Different Sectors of the Economy in Pre-and-Post Period

Period	*Compound growth rate of G.N.P. per annum*	*Primary Sector*	*Secondary Sector*	*Tertiary Sector*
1950-51 to 1964-65	3.85	2.05	6.67	4.87
1964-65 to 1984-85	3.87	2.65	3.97	5.28

In the first period, the higher growth rate of the secondary sector was caused by higher growth rate of industrial output. It was 5.7 per cent in the 1st plan, 7.2 per cent in the second plan and 9.0 per cent in the third plan.

In the second period the higher rate of the tertiary sector was caused by the growth of transport, communication, public administration, defence and banking.

Historically, in the course of the development process, the shares of secondary and tertiary sector in the national income rises and that of the primary sector declines. That has also happened in India.

Year	Share of the primary sector in National Income	Share of Secondary Sector	Share of Tertiary Sector
1950-57	54.4	17.14	24.81
1984-85	37.91	22.17	39.91

But the proportion of labour force engaged in the primary sector has not fallen to the same extent and the share of the labour force in the secondary sector has not increased at all as a evident from Table 11.2.

Table 11.2

Year	% age Share of primary sector in the labour force	% age Share in secondary sector	% age Share of tertiary sector
1950-51	72	11	17
1981	70	13	17

Though there is slight fall in the percentage of people engaged in agriculture, it is still the predominant occupation. Percentage of people engaged in the industrial sector has increased by only two per cent due to smallness of the modern sector and slackening of its rate of growth. The per cent of people engaged in the tertiary sector has remained the same as the spurt in its expansion has reached the limit. Let us now examine the trends in the demand for the different levels and types of education as evident by their respective rates of growth and find out whether there has been balance between needs and demand.

The growth rate of student population of all levels increased from 2.8 crores, in 1950-51 to 11.4 crores in 1982-83 giving a growth rate of 4.5 per cent per annum. The growth rates of different levels of education for the period are given in Table 11.3.

Table 11.3

Levels of Education	Period	Growth rate per Annum	Enrolment Ratio (1982-83)
Primary (6 - 11)	1950-51 to 1982-83	6.2	93.4
Middle (11 - 14)	1950-51 to 1982-83	6.4	48.9

In case of primary education the rate of growth was 6.2 per cent for 1951-61, 5.6 per cent for the period 1961-71 and 2.5 per cent for the period 1971-82. The rate of expansion has slowed down on account of reaching the hard core of school non-attending groups in all states, scheduled caste, scheduled tribes and girls. Further expansion of schooling would depend on socio-economic development of the economically weaker sector of the community.

EDUCATION: SOME PRACTICAL INSIGHTS

Every welfare state provides for its people opportunities for elementary education and primary health care through social sector services. The major thrust of government is to supply social sector output of people free of cost. Table 11.2 depicts the quantum increase in the number of primary schools, secondary schools and colleges in Orissa between 1995-96 and 1999-2000. one feather to the cap of plan exercise in Orissa is the increase in the number of primary schools from 9,801 in 1950-51 to 65,656 in 1999-2000. Today, there is one primary school for every 3.7km. area. Out of the prevailing 65,656 schools, 23,448 are non-formal ones, and the rest are formal schools. The concern of the schools is on creation of a level of awareness among the economically weaker section of the society, through training facilities leading to enhancement of skills of working children.

Plan endeavour in Orissa has embarked on the path of universalisation of elementary education. Universal access and enrolment of children up to 14 years of age in school seems to be instruments in the tool box of universalisation of elementary education progress in this sphere is rather disquieting, because the level of drop-outs at primary level was 43.0 per cent in 1999-2000 as against 43.6 per cent in 1998-99.

The rural-oriented, capital scarce state of Orissa has failed to use economic growth as a basis for transforming the quality of life of people due to prevailing high drop-out ratios in schools for girl child (42.4%), which exceeds the status of male child (40%). The convincing explanation for the underlying tendency of drop-out in schools is, among others, the prevailing high teacher-pupil ratio (1:34 in 1998-99, 1:35 in 1999-2000), which deteriorates the quality of teaching, by making teacher's personal attention of the student difficult.

Table 11.4: Index of Per Capita Real Expenditure on Social Services in Orissa from 1990-91

	Education sports, Arts and Culture			*Medical & Family Health Welfare*			*Social Services*		
	1990-91	95-96	98-99	90-91	95-96	98-99	90-91	95-96	98-99
Orissa	100	115	150	100	106	135	100	120	146

Source: RBI Bulletins.

The phenomenon of one teacher in a school is not strange in Orissa. It is well known that, teaching four to five grades simultaneously requires greater skills. Casual attendance of students, teacher's absenteeism, want of buildings, lack of study materials like maps, globes, books and playgrounds are the villains behind the scene. The recent thrust of the government was on provision of blackboards to enhance the attendance rate of students.

There are close links between nutrition and education. The impact of nutrition on improvement of people's health and learning mentality was borne out by the success, Tamil Nadu achieved in mid-day meals scheme. So, in an effort to achieve the goal of universal elementary education and enhance the nutritional status of children in schools, the government of Orissa has introduced the mid-day-meals programmes in 41,604 primary schools in Orissa (1st July 1995). Stress was laid on enrolment, retention and attendance of students in schools, expectant mothers and children in the age group 6-11 are provided with rice and dal in quantities equivalent to 745 calories. The story of mid-day-meals programme has turned and to be a tale of harbouring hopes and wrinkles of despairs for people of Orissa.

Recently, It has been succinctly observed that, the mid-day-meals scheme could not enhance the nutritional status

Table 11.5: Number of Primary Schools, Students and Teachers in Orissa

Sl. No.	Items	1995-96	1996-97	1997-98	1998-99	1990-2000
1.	Primary schools	56656 42104	65552 42104	65552 42104	65552 42104	65552 42104
	(i) Formal	14552	23448	23448	23448	23448
	(ii) Non-Formal					
2.	Enrolment (In Thousand)	4265	4531	4591	4666	5232
	(i) Formal	3887	3945	4005	4080	4646
	(ii) Non-Formal	378	386	586	586	586
3.	Teachers	125092	134488	134488	134488	135384
	(i) Formal	110540	111040	111040	111040	111040
	(ii) Non-Formal	14552	23448	23448	23448	24344

and attendance rate of students in schools of Kesing Block, because of strategic defect of the scheme, i.e., provision of inferior quality of food to students, in quantities (745 calorie worth for a child) far below the recommended quantity necessary for physical up-keep of the pupil. Further, wastage of time of the pupil was the by-product of cooking arrangements in schools.

Central to the District Primary Education programme, introduced in Orissa in 1996, is the goal of accelerating learning and attendance rate among the students. The scheme attempts to bring tribal dominant, educationally backward districts of Dhenkanal, Bolangir, Gajapati, Rayagada, Bargarh and Sampalbpur districts within the mainstream of development. One, positive sign of progress in higher education profile of the state is, the robust increase in the number of high schools, teachers and students.

THE STATUS OF EDUCATION IN ORISSA AND POLICY PRESCRIPTION

The analysis presented in the forgiving paragraphs reveal that while Orissa has achieved 63.058 per cent literacy rate in 2001, male literacy is brighter than (75.35%) female literacy rate which is 50.51 per cent. There exists yawning gap between general literacy rate on the one hand and literacy rates of tribal and schedule caste population on the other hand. Further, the literacy performance of K.B.K. districts and Phulbani region stands the chances of promising improvement.

There exists scope for rising the state govt. expenditure on education and culture. With a view to making education all inclusive and progressive the government has come forward with the proposal of raising the pay scales of *shikshya sahayaks*. What is tragic about the educational status in Orissa is the presence of one teacher in schools to cover several classes simultaneously.

While there has been impressive quantitative gains in primary and secondary education as reflected in expansion in enrolment ratio, students attendance rate in schools and introduction of mid-day-meals, there has been a progressive decline in the quality of education imparted in schools. The Orissa Development Report 2002 observes that teachers absenteeism in schools in K.B.K. districts is a liability. High teacher pupil ratio, want of study material in schools, payment of regular salaries for school teachers and playgrounds, along with buildings are some areas of concern.

CONCLUSION

From a theoretical stand point, the study has observed that all the principles of estimating the contribution of primary and secondary education for development of an economy should be considered in complementary. Rate of returns from primary education the residual principle, the correlation principle, the correlation principle and demand for and supply sides of education deserves due attention by planners of the state.

One dimension of the educational aspect of human resources development is coordination of research works of different branches of knowledge like Psychology, Education, Economics, Home Science, Science and Commerce faculties.

Upcoming subjects like computer and e-commerce needs an urgent attention. Tribal dialects needs encouragement in tribal schools. Course content of the schools need information and interesting illustrations by the educator to the learner. Human beings are a body-mind-spirit entity, which requires an integral development of these faculties of learning, feeling and action. Music and Drama, Sports and Debates, child to child to learning and a combination of arts education with vocational and science education may perhaps lift the economy of Orissa art of the morals of backwardness and ill health.

To conclude mid-day-meals scheme needs political will and honesty of all concerned for checking misuse of funds.

REFERENCES

1. Prof. D.C. Mishra, Education and Economics Development India, *Orissa Economic Journal,* 1989.
2. Jean Drez and Amartya Sen, *Indians Economic Development*, 1996
3. B. Tilak, Keynote Address, *Indian Economic Association*, Conference Volume, 2005.
4. B. Eswar Rao Pattnaik, *"Education and Health Sectors in Orissa"*, Social Sector Development in India, Raj Kumar Sen Deep & Deep Publication, New Delhi, 2005.
5. *2001 Census*, Government of India.
6. *Economic Survey,* Government of Orissa, Bhubaneswar, 2006-07 and 2007-08.

12

Changing Strategies in Human Resources Management After Globalisation

Santosh Kumar Padhy♣
Rabi. N. Misra♠

INTRODUCTION

A sound macro-economic environment and effective trade polices are essential but not sufficient conditions for integrating developing countries in the multilateral trading system. There is also a need to enhance national and sub national capacity to formulate export strategies at selected product/sector level, grounded on realistic assessments of supply capacities and international demand and an understanding of international commercial practice and standards. To facilitate and support this capacity building, the Government of India, UNCTAD and DFID/UK are jointly implementing a five-year programme titled *"Strategies and Preparedness for Trade and Globalisation in India"*.

♣ Mr. Santosh Kumar Padhy is a Research Scholar, Lecturer in Commerce, K.D. College, Berhampur University.

♠ Dr. Rabi. N. Misra, Professor MBA , SMIT Ankushpur.

Component I of the Project, which is being implemented since March 2003, is already assisting negotiators and policy makers, in enhancing understanding of the development and pro-poor dimension of key trade issues relating to the Doha work programme *Component II* of the programme aims to strengthen human and institutional capacities among stakeholders, as well as a policy environment that will support and sustain a more equitable process of globalisation. *Component II* will facilitate building capacities on trade competitiveness in selected sectors/regions. *Component I* focusses on 'upstream' activities (assisting trade negotiators and policy markers), while *Component II* engages in 'downstream' actions, to build stakeholder capacities for understanding and managing the impact of globalisation on their respective constituencies. The activities under both these components are interlinked, for instance, when research and analysis of negotiating issues (a *Component I* activity) is disseminated to stakeholders and their responses feedback to the negotiators (a *Component II* activity). Although it is not possible to describe a single policy framework that is ideally suited to promoting trade, recent capacity building efforts point to several features or arrangements that have been successful. These include the following:

- A coherent trade strategy that is closely integrated with a country's overall development strategy;
- Effective mechanisms for consultations among the three sets of stakeholders—government, the enterprise and civil society, including trade unions;
- A strategy for enhanced collection, dissemination and analysis of trade related information;
- Trade policy networks supported by indigenous research institutions;
- Networks of trade support institutions;
- A commitment by all key trade stakeholders to 'outward' oriented strategies.

The focus of proposed activities under *Component II* is on strengthening human and institutional capacities of stakeholders and policy makers, to take better-informed decisions, and formulate their strategies with a greater level of understanding of the impact and the opportunities from globalisation, particularly with a pro-poor perspective. To achieve the above objective, *Component II* of the Programme will support activities that enable capacity building of stakeholders that would support:

- ❖ Better understanding and analysis of trade issues, for developing medium term sector strategy;
- ❖ Build institutional and human capacities to deal with existing and emerging trade issues;
- ❖ Disseminate knowledge acquired in the programme widely and deeply in easily digestible language that stakeholders and policy-makers, especially at sub-national level take on board;
- ❖ Provide feedback/inputs to the government to enact sectoral policies; and
- ❖ Schemes focussed on meeting the opportunities and challenges of world trade.

The activities would be prioritised on the basis of their impacts on the poorer and less advantaged sections of the society in the selected sectors. Programme interventions under *Component II* are expected to lead to the following outcomes:

(a) To build stakeholders' institutional and human resource capacities to gain from globalisation, mitigate its negative effects and also influence the planning and policy-making processes. They become outward looking in their orientation. Government agencies have improved understanding of trade issues and this influences required actions from them;

(b) To build national and sub-national core expertise to address the economic implications of the evolving Multilateral Trading System (MTS)-related and Free Trade Agreements (FTAs)-related regulatory/policy framework and formulate negotiating positions on the basis of a good understanding of product and market reality and potential;

(c) To enhance national and sub-national capacity to formulate export strategies at selected product/sector level, grounded on realistic assessments of supply capacities and international demand and an understanding of international commercial practices and standards;

(d) To improve trade performance and facilitate export diversifications in select key product and service sectors. To facilitate international competitiveness at sector level through improved performance at all levels of trade development process by using tools, manuals, guides and opportunities for practical experiences. To strengthen the capacities of trade support institutions to provide effective services to the business community;

(e) To assist in addressing the challenges of increases in imports and the impact it would have on the less competitive domestic firms;

(f) To facilitate engagements among stakeholders to take up policy measures to minimise trade related adjustment costs and to mitigate the short run costs of adjustment, in cases where employment and earnings of the poor have clearly reduced due to increased competition from imports;

(g) Centres of Excellence to analyse effects and opportunities in relation to the selected sectors and selected State;

(h) Research gets disseminated and help those making decisions relating to the sector: politicians,

government officials, industry associations, farmer groups, academia, trade unions, Non Governmental Organisations (NGOs), Panchayati Raj Institutions (PRIs)[1], media;

(i) Media dissemination in mainstream and Indian language covers diverse views of good quality. The activities would be prioritised on the basis of their impacts on the poorer and less advantaged sections of the society in the selected sectors.

An independent consultancy company (Ace Global Private Limited, New Delhi) was appointed to prepare the design of *Component II* based on detailed consultations with various stakeholders.

Objective and Scope

The objective of the study is to highlight the strategies applied during five year programme conducted by the Government of India after 2003 to uplift the poor after Globalisation. Human capacity cannot be changed and opportunities must be provided to achieve the objectives for the purpose only the secondary datas are found in the study.

Programme Activities

The programme would work through a network of stakeholders including private sector, Governments at all levels, civil society organisations, sector bodies and institutions dealing with trade related issues. The success of the programme hinges on the formation and functioning of the sector network with active participation of various stakeholders. The factors in favour of this happening are:

- The programme addresses the real and practical needs of the stakeholders;
- The proposed programme activities will be strictly demand driven;

---

1 These are local self-government institutions at the district, block, and panchayat (village or groups of villages) headed by elected people's representatives.

- ❖ Participation in the sector network by stakeholders will be on a voluntary basis;
- ❖ The involvement of UNCTAD and Ministry of Commerce and Industry, will make the sector network a neutral and credible forum.

The programme expects that *Tier 1* partners would be able to put the sector network in place, and they, along with *Tier 2* partners, would undertake TRCB and other activities, on a demand driven basis. The activities under the programme has a provision for partly meeting the management costs that *Tier 1* and *Tier 2* partners may incur. It would provide such organisations a credible platform to network with all stakeholders, and also access to technical expertise. It is expected that Tier I partners would be able to effectively coordinate with the *Tier 2* partners and other stakeholder bodies. UNCTAD would coordinate with sector partners on a regular basis, and would take on a more proactive role, in partnership with Government, to mobilise the sector stakeholders, should the *Tier 1* partner be not able to put the network in place. An indicative list of the activities that could be taken up under *Component II* of the Project is given below. However, in order to ensure the programme interventions are demand driven, the selected activities would be subject to endorsement by the stakeholders in the sector workshops.

1. Trade related studies, with a pro-poor perspective, for filling information gaps at sector/sub-national and local levels;

2. Sensitisation of the industry and getting their feedback as inputs to the negotiator; for instance:

   - ❖ Potential impact of Market Access of Non Agriculture Products (NAMA) negotiations on domestic producers/exporters;

   - ❖ Impact of Regional Trade Agreements (RTAs)/ Preferential Trade Agreements (PTAs);

- ❖ Impact of tariff peaks and tariff escalation in selected export Markets;
- ❖ Impact of imports on domestic production and consumption, employment, livelihood;
- ❖ Implications of non-tariff barriers such as Sanitary and Phytosanitary (SPS)/Technical Barriers to Trade (TBT) measures.

3. Trade related opportunities and challenges for the poorer sections of the society, particularly in the unorganised and decentralised sub-sectors;
4. Technical assistance, through training programmes, participation in events. Access to ITC tools on trade competitiveness etc;
5. Capacity building for better understanding of trade issues particularly relevant to that sector—
   (a) Market access issues, particularly tariffs;
   (b) Market entry issues, e.g. SPS, standards, regulations;
   (c) Trade defence measures-anti-dumping, subsidies.
6. Increasing the level of awareness about the 'chilling' and other trade defence measures, such as impacts of anti-dumping measures, and assessment of the relative gains to industry from adopting such measures;
7. Outlining specific training and orientation needs for private sector and Government agencies e.g. to understand import market requirements with respect to Rules of Origin and trade facilitation. Funding for such activities will be based on cost-sharing basis;
8. Dissemination of existing studies on trade and other material as well as new content to stakeholders through sector web site, printed newsletters, media reports.

PROGRAMME STRUCTURE

Tier 1 Partner

A vertical structure for each sector selected for the Programme has been adopted as international trade issues impact on a sectoral basis. Each sector has apex organisations dealing with all aspects relating to external trade relating to the sector or sub-sector that they represent. However, the mandate of sector apex bodies is to represent exporters, and their interface is primarily with the last link of the value chain. The value-chain of many export products has linkages in more than one state, and therefore there may be needs for interventions across the value chain, which cannot be undertaken by the sector's apex organisations. To overcome these limitations, The Programme proposes to facilitate the formation of a (virtual) Sector Network of existing national, regional and state level trade related institutions dealing with the respective sectors.

Relationship between Tier 1 and Tier 2 Partners

There would be a close working relationship between *Tier 1* and *Tier 2* partners. All decisions in regard to programme deliverables, time lines, actionable items will get implemented in a mutually consultative process between *Tier 1* and *Tier 2* partners. It is expected that while the broad contours of the activities to be undertaken would be agreed between UNCTAD and *Tier 1* partners, the *Tier 1* and *Tier 2* partners would be jointly responsible for the implementation of these deliverables. *Tier 1* partners would keep UNCTAD informed of the progress in the activities, at least on a monthly basis.

Initial Activities

Formulation and implementation of sound trade development strategies and policies require concerted consultation amongst representatives of three key sets of stakeholders—government at national and sub-national level, enterprise/producers sector and civil society institutions such as trade unions, consumers, environmental and social justice NGOs. Some of the envisaged activities in the first 12 months, by the *Tier 1* partner, in coordination with *Tier 2* partners, are. In order to facilitate the consultation process the programme will help organise workshops at different levels and stages of consultation.

Inception Workshop

An inception workshop shall be held for each sub-sector, organised by respective *Tier 1* partners, with UNCTAD's participation. The objective of this stakeholders' consultation will be to reach agreement on national trade development goals in the sector and a plan to achieve them.

Consultation however is a continuous process and the inception workshop may consider forming a consultative body charged with continuing refinement of trade strategy in response to success, failure and changing circumstances. The consultative body can also be assigned the role of providing guidance on the policies and practices through which the national trade strategy is formulated and implemented in the sector. The group could also coordinate with private sector/ public sector institutions on provision of trade support services. During this workshop, the members would be encouraged to share their knowledge and concerns regarding trade-related issues, and evolve work plans for the Programme (initially covering a one-year duration).

Index

❑❑❑